D0776893

ENDORSEMENTS

Move over Bob Vila! Whether you need a spiritual gut rehab, remodeling, or plain old preventive maintenance, you'll need *this* toolbox by your side. Michelle and John have nailed down practical, easy-to-read blueprints for a man's spiritual growth. Of course we are all "fixer-uppers," but when it comes to spiritual property value for Christian men, location, location, location is still what matters most—and that location is our hearts.

—DR. JEFF BROWN, psychologist, assistant clinical professor at Harvard Medical School, and author of *The Winner's Brain* and *The Runner's Brain*

As an avid do-it-yourselfer, I have acquired an extensive array of tools in my toolbox. I, however, never imagined that there was a whole new way to look at my toolbox until I read *God Glimpses from the Toolbox: Living as Men of Character and Strength*. Reading this book has shown me that just as I am careful about using the proper tools when doing improvements to my home, I need to equip myself with the proper spiritual tools as well as know how to correctly use them if I am to make much-needed improvements to my spiritual home. What great lessons I learned and can now apply to my life through this marvelous book! Excuse me now as I go plan my next do-it-yourself project.

—ISAAC HERNANDEZ, VP of Programming at Parables TV

We built our home so we have tools upon tools we used to build a strong and stable home. That same plethora of handy tools is exactly what John Perrodin and Michelle Cox have placed in *God Glimpses from the Toolbox: Living as Men of Character and Strength*. Having three sons and a grandson, this book is exactly the kind of toolbox every guy needs to hammer together a sturdy and well-built future.

—PAM AND BILL FARREL, authors of forty-five books, including
7 Simple Skills for Every Woman
and *7 Simple Skills for Every Man*

Catching a glimpse of God is one of the great joys and encouragements in our daily walk with the Lord. I'm so glad Michelle and John wrote the *God Glimpses* books. It's a brilliant concept—stuffing jewelry boxes and toolboxes with clever concepts to enhance our relationship with God.

—TODD STARNES, FOX News & Commentary

You can't do better than my friends Michelle Cox and John Perrodin if you're looking for spiritual guidance leading to real growth. When I think of them both, what comes to mind—beyond their commitment to stellar writing and careful scriptural scholarship—is a deep love for God and a reverence for His Word. Add to that their examples as spouses and parents in two long-term marriages, and you have a pair of authors uniquely qualified to mine the unsearchable riches of Christ. Immerse yourself in *God Glimpses* ... and come away more disciplined, consistent, and prepared to serve.

—JERRY B. JENKINS, novelist and biographer, JerryJenkins.com

What a clever idea! I like the use of "manly" stuff as a way to illustrate our relationship with God.

—KEN RANEY, Clash Entertainment

GOD GLIMPSES

from the

TOOL BOX

LIVING AS MEN OF CHARACTER AND STRENGTH

JOHN PERRODIN
and MICHELLE COX

BroadStreet
PUBLISHING

BroadStreet Publishing Group, LLC
Racine, Wisconsin, USA
BroadStreetPublishing.com

GOD GLIMPSES FROM THE TOOLBOX
LIVING AS MEN OF CHARACTER AND STRENGTH

ISBN-13: 978-1-4245-5211-5 (hardcover)
ISBN-13: 978-1-4245-5212-2 (e-book)

Quotes from the authors are so identified. Quotes in chapters 2–3, 6–7, 9–10, 15, 17–18, 20, 23, 26–27, and 29 are taken from Worth Repeating © 2003 by Bob Kelly. Published by Kregel Publications, Grand Rapids, MI. Used by permission of the publisher. All rights reserved. All other quotes are in the public domain and sourced with appreciation to www.bartelby.com.

Scripture quotations are taken from the King James Version of the Bible.

Stock or custom editions of BroadStreet Publishing titles may be purchased in bulk for educational, business, ministry, fundraising, or sales promotional use. For information, please e-mail info@broadstreet publishing.com.

Cover design by Chris Garborg, garborgdesign.com
Interior design and typesetting by Katherine Lloyd, TheDESKonline.com

Printed in China

16 17 18 19 20 5 4 3 2 1

I wish to dedicate this book to the queen of my heart, Sue, and my four princesses: Jenna, Carol, Cosette, and Liesl, through whom I am daily granted glimpses of God's love and blessings. I also want to thank my team of mighty men who have helped me with more projects and planning than I can possibly list: Jace, Patch, Quentin, Tad, Tom, Mark, Wade, Jackson, Paul, Bill, Bob, Brian, Bruce, Doug, Derek, Rob, and Ed.

JOHN PERRODIN

This book is dedicated to my little buddies— my grandsons Jack, Ethan, and Nolan. My prayer is that you'll find glimpses of God in every day, and that as you grow up, you'll use God's tools to become men of character. Grandmama loves you!

MICHELLE COX

Iron sharpeneth iron;
so a man sharpeneth
the countenance of his friend.

—*Proverbs 27:17*

CONTENTS

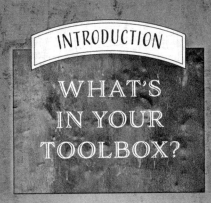

INTRODUCTION

WHAT'S IN YOUR TOOLBOX?

Guys, what's in your toolboxes? Most of us have hammers and screwdrivers for home repairs. Tools for demo work. And power tools—because nothing brings greater happiness than making messes and generating *lots* of noise.

We'll admit that sometimes we don't use the best judgment when we do things. Proof of that can be found in blackened nails where we've hit our thumbs instead of the boards, bruises we wear as badges of honor, and cuts we've received from sharp pieces of metal. Yes, we keep the bandage folks in business!

When we look into our toolboxes, it's easy to see the items that are in there. But what most of us haven't discovered before are the amazing spiritual lessons hiding between the pliers and the wrenches.

Glimpses of God are present in every aspect of our lives if we'll just open our eyes and look around. That's the premise for the *God Glimpses* book series: to take important spiritual truths and apply them to ordinary experiences, such as the items found in a toolbox or jewelry box, a visit to the gym, or a day in the garden. We *can* discover God's will and purpose for our lives if we'll just take time to catch a glimpse of Him.

God often mentions tools and building in the Bible. Jesus spent His childhood with His earthly father as Joseph shared his knowledge of carpentry and building skills. Men used tools to construct the cross and then drove nails into the hands and feet of our Savior as He hung on that rugged tree. How appropriate then, that *God Glimpses from the Toolbox: Living as Men of Character and Strength* is an inspirational book for men featuring the tools found in a toolbox.

Each of the chapters includes a definition of a tool and the spiritual application gleaned from it. Then, inspirational stories feature an anecdote about building, followed by a quote, a prayer, and a verse of Scripture that hammers home the truths of each chapter. A "building permit" page (asking, "What will I permit God to do in *my* life?") provides thought-provoking questions at the end of each chapter.

Guys, we don't know about you, but we want to be powered up and ready for God to use our lives. We want to be dependable tools in His toolbox. Please join us as we look for God glimpses from the toolbox.

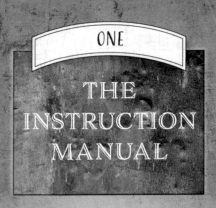

ONE

THE INSTRUCTION MANUAL

Reading the instruction manual will assist the builder in knowing how to use the tools properly, how to care for the tools, and how to use them safely in conjunction with the manufacturer's instructions or OSHA-mandated rules. But the instruction manual doesn't do any good unless it is read and put to use. Failure to utilize the instructions can lead to delays, injuries, and additional costs, so a wise man will begin each job by following the directions.

It won't kill a guy to follow instructions,
but it just might kill him if he doesn't.

—Michelle Cox

Just Follow the Instructions

"What are we going to cook first? Steaks? Mile-high burgers? Hot dogs with all the trimmings?" Whoops of excitement filled the air as Keith asked those questions. He and his buddies were out on his deck for a momentous occasion.

Keith had owned a cheap grill, but he'd just gotten the mack daddy of all grills as his Father's Day gift. This baby was sweet! Gleaming stainless steel. An extra-large cooking surface. Two side burners. Hooks for hanging grill tools. A halogen light. It even had a smoker box to flavor the meat.

Keith felt almost as if he needed a moment of silence. He couldn't wait for that first bite of awesomeness from his grill, but there was one small obstacle—it wasn't assembled. That's where his buddies came in.

Using a utility knife, they slit the box, dumping the grill pieces on the deck. They worked as a team, assembling the parts, fitting nuts and bolts together, tightening everything with their wrenches and other tools until a shiny grill appeared before their eyes.

There was a problem, however. It didn't work. And there were several leftover parts. The men tried fitting the extra pieces into place, but they didn't fit right, and the grill still didn't work.

Then one of the guys did something unusual. Some-

thing most men avoid at all costs. He picked up the manual and read the instructions. "I think I see the problem. There's a piece we were supposed to install when we started assembling the grill. We're going to have to take most of the grill apart and go back and do that. It's the only way we can fix the problem."

Everyone groaned. Dinner would be delayed—because they hadn't followed the instructions. Man, if they'd only read the manual, they'd already be filling their plates with thick slabs of steak. They'd messed up for sure.

But isn't that exactly what we do spiritually? God has sent us an instruction manual in His Word. It tells us exactly what to do, what to avoid, and who will cause us problems, and it even spells out the consequences for not following His instructions.

Then we go out following our own plans—and we mess up. We ruin relationships. We go places and look at things we shouldn't. We do stupid things.

All of a sudden, we realize our life isn't going right, that there are problems. Sometimes we even try to fix those situations ourselves—and often cause even more heartache and difficulties.

Pull out God's instruction manual. Read the directions and make the necessary repairs. Spare your loved ones the heartache of a man who failed God's plan for his life.

The solution is so simple: just follow the instructions.

All scripture is given by inspiration of God,
and is profitable for doctrine, for reproof,
for correction, for instruction in righteousness:
That the man of God may be perfect, thoroughly
furnished unto all good works.
—*2 Timothy 3:16–17*

Dear Father, I don't know why I'm always so bull-headed and insist on doing things my way, or think I can help you fix whatever is going on in my life. Help me to remember that you can build me into a better man if I'll get out of the way and let you be in charge. Thank you for being a God of patience and love. Remind me to read the directions in your Word and to allow you to show me the plans you have for me. In the midst of my busy days, help me to make time to talk with you. I want to be a man of character, a man who follows after you in everything he does. Amen.

THE BUILDING PERMIT PAGE

WHAT WILL I PERMIT GOD TO DO IN MY LIFE?

1. Just as Keith and his buddies messed up the grill assembly because they didn't read the instructions, we can cause havoc in our lives when we don't follow the instructions found in God's Word. Why do we do that? What steps can we take to become more consistent about Bible study time?

2. How does it impact our attitudes, influence, and relationships when we aren't spending time with God? How does it affect those things when we do spend time with Him?

3. We often forget that other people are watching us to see how we live each day. What do others observe when they look at you? What would you like for them to see?

4. What plan does God have for your life? What would you like to accomplish for Him?

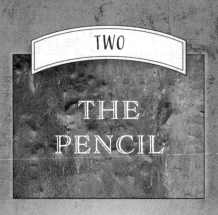

TWO

THE PENCIL

The pencil seems so minor compared to all the other tools in the toolbox, yet it is indispensable to the builder. It often wears down, but it can be sharpened again. By the time the contractor finishes building a house, the pencil has touched almost every piece of wood in the structure. Just as the pencil leaves its mark on the wood, we leave our mark on every person with whom we come in contact.

❄

I am like a little pencil in God's hand.
He does the writing.
—*Mother Teresa*

A Vital Tool

A pencil inside a toolbox seems insignificant next to a hammer, wrenches, and other hefty items. Most people probably wouldn't even notice it—but the contractor knows it's vital.

The cool thing about the pencil is that it doesn't matter if the builder is using it for an 800-square-foot starter home or a 20,000-square-foot mansion, it's still up to the task.

Dave builds custom houses. When looking over blueprints, he uses a pencil to figure out how much wood he'll need to build the house. When the pencil gets dull, he just sharpens it again and it's good to go.

Sometimes Dave makes notes of things he needs to remember on the blueprints. A pencil works great because he can erase those reminders when using the same plans for another house.

When Dave and his crew start building the home, the true value of that pencil comes into play. You see, the builder uses that simple pencil to mark the pieces of wood so he will know where to cut them. By the time the house is built, that pencil will have touched every piece of wood in that home. Important job, wouldn't you say?

That reminds me of when I was on a construction team that went to Costa Rica to help some missionaries. Our group attended church with them on the Sunday we were

there. During his sermon, the minister told about another group from the United States who'd attended their service the week before.

He shared about one of the young men who was an artist. The pastor said, "He took a pencil and started making some lines, and soon a beautiful picture appeared."

Just like the pencil that Dave uses when he builds houses, and the one that the artist used for his artwork, God wants us to make our mark on the world for Him. We might not see the blueprints for what He has planned for us, but as we serve Him each day, something beautiful will begin to show.

I don't know about you, but sometimes I let my insecurities keep me from doing things for Him. But like that pencil in the hand of the builder, we just need to be available for Him to use us.

It's easy to get busy with life and our families and lose our focus on serving Him, becoming worn down or even broken. Is that where you are right now? Then spend time in His Word and in prayer. Sharpen your soul so you'll be ready to work for Him.

Allow God to use your life—whether it's a small task, like that 800-square-foot home, or something huge, like that 20,000-square-foot mansion. Become a pencil in the hand of a big God, and let Him build you into a man of purpose.

For we are his workmanship, created in Christ Jesus unto good works, which God hath before ordained that we should walk in them.
—*Ephesians 2:10*

Lord, sometimes I feel so insignificant as I look at others who are more successful. I'm so grateful, though, that just like that simple pencil, you can still use my life. Help me to spend time in your Word so my faith will be sharpened. Remind me to set aside quiet time so I can talk with you and listen to what you want to tell me. Thank you for your grace that erases my failures. As I go about each day, help me to leave marks behind that will draw folks to you. Make me a faithful pencil in your mighty hand, and build me into a man of purpose and integrity. Amen.

THE BUILDING PERMIT PAGE

WHAT WILL I PERMIT GOD TO DO IN MY LIFE?

1. The pencil seems so insignificant, yet it is vital to the builder. Do you ever feel insignificant spiritually? What are some ways that God can use your life for valuable purposes?

2. When the pencil becomes worn down, it must be sharpened before it's useful again. What do you need to do to be sharp for God?

3. The pencil touches every piece of wood in a house. How are you touching the lives of others for Him?

4. Look back at your spiritual journey and think about some ways God has made something beautiful out of your life. Write down three of those things, then spend some time thanking Him.

THREE

THE TAPE MEASURE

A tape measure is a flexible tape marked off in a scale, and it's used for taking measurements and determining size. Some tapes are expandable to 300-plus feet. The workman's measuring tape is a metal strip that is easily contained within a pocket or toolbox. The tape should be bendable but also rigid enough to measure long distances without sagging. Because it isn't solid like a yardstick, the tape measure can be used to gauge measurements around corners or curves.

The way a man measures up to God's expectations
isn't by accumulating possessions—but more by
spending time on his knees with heartfelt confessions.
—*Michelle Cox*

THE MEASURE OF A HEART

Measurements matter. They're the only way you can build to spec. And such careful design is how you end up making a doghouse and not a mother-in-law suite. (And if you don't make the second one exceptionally well, you may end up in the first!) Details must be reviewed and written down and all measurements carefully calculated. Most guys need to take the time to calculate more than once, just to be sure that the numbers didn't somehow slip, slide, or switch spots.

Having the big picture in mind is important. Goals keep us moving ahead. We want to be a part of something grand, something that matters—even if we're just making a birdhouse. Granted, there's often a difference between what's in our heads and what ends up being built. Often adjustments must be made to our blueprints midway, but having things set out in writing and with specific measurements helps keep us on track.

When it comes to a measuring tape, we want the kind that snaps to attention but zips out of the way when we've made our marks. That tape is like a temporary guide that we can call on when needed, then it disappears. We know it's there, but we don't have to keep it open. Realizing it's available is enough. In the same way, we have a history with our tools. We trust them to be available when we need them.

The Bible is like that. We have special verses memorized, but we know that we can always go back to the Book and open it when we want to check on something important. We should also remember that God is always there for us.

As Christians, we must be specific about setting out the details that matter. Otherwise we may find ourselves sinking hours into a project that has no real purpose. Counting the cost isn't just about having the money to finish a task. We also need the time and energy required to complete the goals we've committed to.

When it comes to measuring a man's heart, some guys are better at showing their feelings than others. However, one of the real ways to see what's inside a man is to observe how he treats those he claims to love, especially in the spontaneous moments. When you see him open a door for his wife or steal a quick kiss, you realize that his love isn't for show.

How we measure up in God's eyes is what matters most—not what others think of us. And each of us is responsible for our own choices and decisions. When we count our accomplishments, do we discover that we're doing all that we can for the kingdom? When God whips out His measuring tape and wraps it around our hearts, what will He find?

A new heart also will I give you and
a new spirit will I put within you: and I will
take away the stony heart out of your flesh,
and I will give you an heart of flesh.

—*Ezekiel 36:26*

*Lord, sometimes I feel like I've got the Grinch's
"before" heart. I am not always as open and gener-
ous as I should be. Perhaps it's the weight of all my
worries that hardens my heart. But I don't want to
be that way. I want a soft heart toward you, toward
my loved ones, and toward those who are unsaved.
Please forgive me for taking things so personally,
for the times I respond defensively instead of with
logic and self-control. Help me to see things from
a different perspective and to offer encouragement
and hope, especially to those who disagree with
me. I want to be your man. Take the measure of my
heart and make it yours. Amen.*

THE BUILDING PERMIT PAGE

WHAT WILL I PERMIT GOD TO DO IN MY LIFE?

1. Being a man in today's world is a tough job. We're expected to be strong but sensitive. I admit it—I don't always get the balance right. What are some areas where you need to make adjustments?

2. Having the big picture in mind is important in a building project and also spiritually. Think of three goals you'd like to achieve for God.

3. Just as a measuring tape is available when needed on the jobsite, God is always available for us. Think of some times when God was there when you needed Him.

4. When you stand before the Lord one day and He pulls out the judgment tape, how will your heart measure up? What do you need to do to improve those results?

27

FOUR

THE BAND CLAMPS

Clamps are devices for holding objects and fastening them together, and they're often used for welding, woodworking, and automotive projects. They come in a variety of styles and sizes. Band (or web) clamps allow a furniture builder to tightly grip multiple items whose surfaces are not parallel to one another. An example would be clamping the staves of a barrel—a flexible band clamp would encircle all the individual pieces. Pressure is then applied by ratcheting down the webbed band slowly.

Where others look at us and see a mess,
God looks at us and sees potential.

—Michelle Cox

CAUGHT IN A VISE

An antique chair sits in a heap, back slats askew, armrests akimbo, legs scattered like firewood. The inexperienced buyer would have but one verdict: hopeless. Kindling at best. At first glance, it looks like a 3-D puzzle with every piece broken or bent.

Thankfully, the antique buyer sees more. His well-trained eye sees past the immediate problems and imagines the potential. After putting down his money, he bundles the strips of cherry and hauls the pile to the wood shop for an estimate.

"Got a real mess there," the man says, coming around the counter. His coarse fingertips stroke the smooth armrest. Clearly, this craftsman knows good wood when he sees it. Scratching his head, he imagines the master of the house sitting at the head of the table, leading the mealtime prayer.

Slight indents have formed where elbows dug in for decades. "Gonna cost you plenty. Time, labor, materials." He pauses, "But she'll be a beauty when I'm done."

Slowly, carefully, the old man takes stock of what's salvageable and what needs to be sanded, reshaped, or created from scratch. It's going to be work—but worth every bead of sweat. When he has the pieces ready, he dollops glue on them and fits them together. He wraps strong canvas bands

around the pieces to hold them in place. He goes slowly, carefully, section by section, first the back, then the legs and seat. The armrests are added last.

The band clamps are loose at first, but properly placed. This is crucial. Tighter, tighter, tighter the ratchet squeezes down, simultaneously pulling in and on the strips of fabric. Glue oozes, and the man wipes the excess. There's more pressure to come. "Just needs some rest now," he says absently.

Chair repairs can seem costly, especially if a customer doesn't understand the delicacy required to bring disparate pieces together. Slowly, carefully, but all at once. Proper timing is as crucial as a gentle touch. And much experience. Never trust a treasure to an amateur unless you want to be sorely disappointed.

When God works on broken hearts or tattered lives, most of us prefer a miraculous wand wave to the slow clamping-down process. Both work, but God usually takes His time. A master craftsman knows not to rush. He ratchets down one tooth, then the next, then the next.

The tightening seems unbearable. We long for our former disorder to this rigid rehab. But for healing to take root, we need to accept. Then rest. With the restored pieces correctly in place, we can only wait. Otherwise, we might warp or even snap and break—and be in worse shape than before the process began.

Clamps come in many shapes and sizes. We can choose to ignore the pain and pressure—or embrace it. The wise ask God to use the clamps He must to accomplish the lasting repairs we need.

I drew them with cords of a man,
with bands of love.

—Hosea 11:4

Lord, I want instant results, but you already know that about me. The idea of slow pressure applied for days, months, or even years scares me. I don't even like waiting to fill up my truck at the gas station! But I have seen the results of such patience in the lives of others—and yes, even in my own. Please show me the broken parts in my life and relationships that need fixing. In truth, I am still a little boy in need of the caring compassion of my Father. Cover me, enfold me with your gentle loving bands and bring me back to a place of wholeness. Help me to withstand your healing hug with a willing heart. Amen.

THE BUILDING PERMIT PAGE

WHAT WILL I PERMIT GOD TO DO IN MY LIFE?

1. What's the biggest mistake you've ever made? What have you done to prevent another mess from happening in the future?

2. Did you turn your obvious mistakes over to the Lord or try to fix things yourself? Why is it so easy to fall into patterns that you know will bring the same results?

3. What are some basic ways that God sees you differently than you see yourself? Do you ever give yourself a break and realize that you are loved even when you're extremely unlovable?

4. What attitudes do you need to change to allow God to mend your heart? Do you often have trouble even acknowledging that something is your problem? Have you asked God to open your eyes to ways that you can serve others?

FIVE

THE SCREW-DRIVER

A screwdriver is a tool used to twist screws into a surface, thereby connecting two objects together. Interestingly, the process works best if there's a small nail hole for the tip of the screw to rest in. That starting point matters. The screwdriver's sturdy tip fits into the head of a screw, and the body is made of steel for strength and durability. The popular Phillips screwdriver provides great torque and tighter fastening because the cross-shaped tip of the driver wedges perfectly into the crosshead screw.

May I govern my passion with absolute sway,
And grow wiser and better
as my strength wears away.
—Walter Pope

FEELING THE PRESSURE

The relationship between the screw and screwdriver is not a democracy. The man with the hand on the driver decides where and how deep to place the screw. And the hapless screw has scarce opportunity to change things. The history of the screwdriver is intriguing, and the partnership between tool and fastener was unworkable until technological advances made it possible to melt metal cheaply and cast the indispensable screws. But once developed, they became vital to construction projects of all sizes.

The screwdriver itself requires hand, finger, forearm, and shoulder strength to gain the leverage necessary to propel the screw deep into wood. It went through transformations of its own, morphing from "turn-handle" to convenient electric or battery-powered devices.

As simple and elegant as the screwdriver is, there are some basic rules to using it successfully. First, make sure to match the type of screw—typically a flathead/slotted screw or a crosshead/Phillips-head screw—to the type of screwdriver. The screwdriver tip must also match the size of the screw. If you try to use a flathead screwdriver for a Phillips-head, it will slip. And if you use a wrong-sized screwdriver tip, it won't fit or will slip and won't turn efficiently, if at all.

The cross shape of the Phillips-head screwdriver tip is a

simple reminder that Jesus paid the ultimate price to fasten us to Him. With a careful hand, He reaches into our hearts and heads, carefully attaching us to prevent slippage.

But how often do we live our life in such a way that we fight against the plans God has for us? Instead of submitting to His will and purpose, we push back. We numb our conscience. We refuse to do what He wants because we think we know better.

The similarity between God's Holy Spirit and the simple, powerful screwdriver is powerful. The Spirit knows exactly what shape we are in and when and how to prompt and prod and even put pressure on us. God's straightforward love is seen in the way the Spirit drives us toward holiness.

The next time you heft a screwdriver in your hand and prepare to do battle with a screw that needs to be put into its proper place, think about your own life. Consider the times when you have detoured from God's path, rejected possibilities for evangelism, or disregarded an opportunity to tunnel more deeply into Scripture.

God is good. All the time. You'll never get more than you can bear. Beware, though. He knows your deep inner strength and will prompt you and push you to grow, to become a holy man of God. Like it or not.

As obedient children, not fashioning yourselves according to the former lusts in your ignorance: But as he which hath called you is holy, so be ye holy in all manner of conversation; Because it is written, Be ye holy; for I am holy.

—*1 Peter 1:14–16*

Precious Lord, some guys are handier with tools than others. There are times when I feel as if the tools in my box are out to get me. Take the screwdriver. I know you're not supposed to use it to pry things open, dig weeds out of concrete cracks, or turn the handle into a hammer, but I do sometimes. I try to make things work, to force things. Take the easy way. Father, I know I've often done the same with you. Please keep moving me in the right direction. Closer to you. Keep opening up opportunities for growth; keep pushing me to become the holy man of God that you desire me to be. And though I'm never going to build a cabin from hand—I struggle to pound together a simple bird feeder—you still love me. Thank you, Lord. Amen.

THE BUILDING PERMIT PAGE

WHAT WILL I PERMIT GOD TO DO IN MY LIFE?

1. Hand tools remind us about the state of our strength. Do you believe God can use a man no matter what age he is? Think about some examples you've seen from life and Scripture.

2. A screwdriver is worthless without a screw. How do we work better in tandem with God to accomplish anything—including great things?

3. It takes strength to drive a screw into something. Why do you think it's important for us to be strong spiritually?

4. The builder puts pressure on the screw to drive it into place. God sometimes uses pressure to drive us to Him. What have you learned from those pressure-filled moments of your life?

SIX

THE HANDSAW

A handsaw is a portable cutting tool having a flexible metal blade with a sharp-toothed edge. It takes strength to use a handsaw. Its primary use is for simple cutting work, and it can also remove imperfections. The builder holds the saw in one hand and stabilizes the piece of wood with the other hand, but care must be taken to avoid injuries from the sharp teeth of the blade.

God takes hold when we break down.
We go as far as we can and then God takes
hold when we can't go any farther.

—A. P. Gouthey

GOD'S BUILDING PROJECT

Three-year-old Bobby picked up his play tool set. He strapped on the tool belt with its hammer, screwdriver, pliers, and wrench, and then he grabbed his plastic handsaw and a piece of wood. "Daddy, I'm gonna make a shelf for Mommy."

"She'll like that, buddy."

Bobby made buzzing noises as he used the tools. They were his favorite toys, and he'd spent numerous hours working on "pwojects" as his daddy built or repaired things.

He worked industriously with his plastic handsaw, but even though he worked hard, the board didn't take shape like it did when his daddy used a saw.

Several years later, Bobby's dad bought him a small handsaw that would actually cut wood. He warned his son, "Don't use this except when I'm with you." And then he gave Bobby a few safety rules so he wouldn't get cut by the sharp teeth on the saw.

Bobby was excited. He grabbed his saw and started cutting a board. But there were a couple of problems—he didn't have the strength to hold the saw and wood steady. The cut was crooked and rough, made worse by an imperfection that needed to be removed from the board.

Seeing Bobby's dejected face, his dad walked over. "Son,

I'm going to put my hand on yours so you can have some of my strength. Let's do this together."

And with the touch of his father's hand, Bobby removed the imperfection, cutting until the once-jagged board was smooth and straight.

Our lives are much like little Bobby's. We start our Christian walk with immaturity, and then—if we spend time in prayer and God's Word—we mature, gaining wisdom and strength that allows us to accomplish the big tasks God has for us to do.

But often the imperfections in our lives have to be cut away by our Father, each sawblade of conviction cutting into our hearts, our jagged edges smoothed out by His love and grace.

Even then, there are times when we go through difficult circumstances or we attempt to do things for Him and we cry out, "God, I don't have the strength to do this."

And we don't. But when our Father places His strong hand on our lives, we can accomplish the task through *His* strength.

That's the question for all of us: Are we playing at our faith—like young Bobby was with his play tool set—or are we becoming strong men of faith? The answer to that question is important if we want to please God—and if we want to be a good example for the little eyes that are watching us just as Bobby watched his dad.

For I the LORD thy God will hold thy right hand,
saying unto thee, Fear not; I will help thee.
—Isaiah 41:13

Lord, life is too important for me to spend my time just playing at it. I don't want to remain a child spiritually. I want to grow in my faith and become a true man of God for you. Even though it's sometimes painful, cut out the imperfections that keep me from being what you want me to be. I know my strength is limited, but I'm so grateful that your strength is limitless. Remind me often that other eyes—especially those little eyes—are watching me to see how I live each day. Help them to see a man who's been shaped by the Master Builder's hands. Amen.

THE BUILDING PERMIT PAGE

WHAT WILL I PERMIT GOD TO DO IN MY LIFE?

1. Bobby's dad gave him safety rules when he bought his son the real saw. God has given us safety rules for life and they're found in the Bible. What are three things you can do to protect yourself from wrong decisions?

2. Just as young Bobby couldn't use the new saw under his own strength, our power can be found in God. Write about a time you went to Him for strength.

3. Sometimes the builder has to cut away imperfections before he can use a piece of wood. What imperfections in your life are keeping you from becoming the man God wants you to be?

4. It's easy to forget that other people are watching us. What do you hope they see when they look at you?

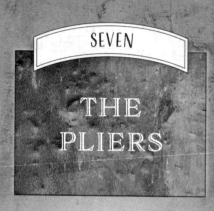

SEVEN

THE PLIERS

Pliers are tools that have a pair of pivoted jaws used for holding, bending, cutting, or shaping many types of construction materials. They strengthen a man's grip. Mechanics and sheet metal workers sometimes consider pliers to be their third hand. Locking pliers securely wedge things in place until the hand of the builder releases it. A mechanic relies on locking pliers to keep the focus of his work directly in front of him.

Have a purpose in life, and having it,
throw into your work such strength of mind
and muscle as God has given you.
—*Thomas Carlyle*

HOLDING ON TIGHTLY

Like scissors, pliers come in pairs. And each set makes one incredibly useful tool for holding, twisting, and cutting away unneeded parts and pieces. Think about that old bent nail stuck in the plaster. Pliers help you pop out the protruding piece quickly without causing unnecessary damage. The fulcrum, the point where the lever rests, allows the jaws of the pliers to shut tightly and exponentially increase a man's grip strength.

Different pliers have different purposes. Long-nosed and flat-nosed pliers can reach into small places that are too constricted for thick fingers. Utility pliers in all shapes and sizes allow a man to get a grip—literally—on things where wrenches are too finicky to attach. Various types of cutting pliers do as their name implies: they snip wires, pins, nails, and fasteners. Of course, to be most effective, they must be sharp. As we all know, the sharpest pliers cut best and fastest.

God's purposes and plans for us are similar. Often we decide on a whim what we think we are meant to do. Not bothering to check in with our Maker first, we determine we should cut, grab, or probe messy situations that we have no business touching. Consider how many times we've quickly and incorrectly drawn conclusions before taking our questions to the Lord. Such prayer-free thinking rarely turns out well.

We need to stay sharp and discerning. We've got to be sure our choices are fully informed by the holy Word of God. That's what the Bible is for, not as Sunday-only reading material or something to clutter the coffee table. Rather than pretending we know it all, we should pray for the continued and continuous flow of the Holy Spirit.

Through Him we have our strength. He allows us to walk in courage. But often we stumble ahead, doing whatever seems easiest, when we should be waiting for God's answer to fervent prayer.

A common admonition that applies to pliers as well as many other tools is this: don't use them as a stand-in for a hammer. The temptation is great when we've got such a handy multipurpose tool at hand. Why not just use it to bash a nail into place or maybe force a bolt tighter? Here's why: because such misuse can cause damage to the tool and possibly us too.

God doesn't want us to force-fit simple solutions to complex situations. Sure, pliers sometimes work. So we grab them whether or not they are really right for the job. Spiritually speaking, though, shortcuts are rarely a good idea. God's purposes are completed in His perfect timing, and His plan is always best. It's up to us to decide if we have the courage to wait on the Lord or insist on jamming things through—ready or not.

Even for this same purpose have I raised thee up,
that I might shew my power in thee, and that my
name might be declared throughout all the earth.
—Romans 9:17

*Dear God, sometimes I need you to take those
heavenly pliers and grab hold of the things that
are pushing down on me. I have buried myself with
so many demands that I've forgotten the joy and
creativity that comes from being your child. I know
there are layers of guilt welded to my mind, my
body, and my soul. That's why I must have your
healing help. It's a simple truth: I can't free myself by
myself. Please remind me I can have your forgiveness each and every day. You want me to unburden
myself and not be hunched over with worldly
weights and unhealthy expectations. Show me how
to be free—pried free if necessary—from the stuff
that has no part of a God-blessed heart. I know you
have a purpose and plan for me. Help me to live
your purpose instead of mine. Amen.*

THE BUILDING PERMIT PAGE

WHAT WILL I PERMIT GOD TO DO IN MY LIFE?

1. Do you like to sit still? In what circumstances does God need to hold you down with a pair of His pliers to get you to listen to Him?

2. When using cutting pliers, you want them to be sharp. How can you be sharp for God? What traits do you need to accomplish that?

3. Have you ever used pliers to free something from a place it doesn't belong? Reflect on how God has pulled you out of some genuine messes—and thank Him!

4. Just as there is a purpose for each type of pliers, God has a purpose and plan for us. Think of a time when you went after your own plan instead of God's. What did you learn from that experience?

EIGHT

THE TROWEL

A trowel is a hand tool for leveling, spreading, or shaping substances such as cement. Tile setters use them for grouting, and gardeners use them for lawn work. They are a must-have tool for brick masons as they build fireplaces, chimneys, and new foundations. Like the tile setters and the gardeners, the brick mason has a reputation to maintain, and he will work hard to keep a good name in the community where he works.

Character is like the foundation of a house—
it is below the surface.

—*Anonymous*

FLEXIBLE FOR GOD

Paul is a brick mason. His tools are an important part of all that he does, and one of his most indispensable tools is his trowel. But not just any trowel will do. There are different sizes and shapes of trowels, and the masonry contractor buys the one that will work best.

Paul has a favorite brand that he uses, and whenever he buys a new trowel, he makes sure he buys the same brand. It's worth the cost to him. He's tried others, but they are sometimes not limber enough. If they're too stiff, they're not easy to work with, making his job harder.

It's also important for him to make the mortar the right consistency. If it's too thick, it won't spread well. If it's too thin, it will slide or drip off the trowel and the bricks.

Paul uses the trowel to scoop up the mortar from the mortar board. He's been a mason for long enough that he knows just how much he needs. He takes the mortar and butters it onto the bricks with the trowel, smoothing it out where it needs to go so the bricks will join tightly together, providing strength and permanence.

Sometimes Paul uses his trowel to cut brick. Again, he's done this job for so many years that he knows exactly how to hit the brick so that he'll get the cut where he needs it. And at the end of every workday, it's important for Paul to clean his trowel well so that it's ready to use when the next task comes along.

It's the same with our spiritual lives. Just as Paul purchased his favorite brand of trowel, God purchased us—at the cost of His own life. But He considers us well worth it.

He wants His children to be pliable and tender to His leading and to be available for Him to use. But sometimes we haven't cleaned our hearts and we aren't ready when He has a task for us to do. And like that stiff trowel, some of us greet Him with hardened hearts instead of tender ones—and He isn't able to use our lives as well.

The Master Builder knows just how much testing or hardship to put into our lives to make us reliable for Him. Just as the mason sometimes has to cut the bricks with the trowel, God knows what we need to cut from our lives so He can smooth us and join our hearts tightly—permanently—with Him.

And that brings us to the question for all of us who long to be men of character: Are our hearts the equivalent of that stiff trowel, or are they tender and pliable, available for Him to use?

And whatsoever ye do, do it heartily,
as to the Lord, and not unto men.
—*Colossians 3:23*

Dear Father, just as the builder wants a good reputation in the community, give me a reputation as a man whose heart longs to please you. Help me to be pliable and tender so you can use me. Thank you for the trials and hardships you've sent my way. I'll be the first to admit that I didn't like them, but they taught me to trust you in a way I wouldn't have done otherwise, to place my life and everyone I love in your hands. Cut what doesn't need to be there out of me. Just as the mason builds a beautiful brick wall or fireplace, build me into a man of steadfast character, a man who will follow you all the days of his life. Amen.

THE BUILDING PERMIT PAGE

WHAT WILL I PERMIT GOD TO DO IN MY LIFE?

1. What kind of reputation do you have? How can you be intentional about leaving behind the legacy of a man who loved God?

2. It's never fun to go through hard times, but they help to build us into strong Christians. Think about a difficult time you went through. What did you learn from it?

3. Just as the mason has to make the mortar the right consistency, we must be careful about what we put into our lives each day. How are you doing with keeping the right balance in your career, your family, and serving God?

4. The mason doesn't want a trowel that's stiff and inflexible. When we're stiff and inflexible, God can't use our lives to the fullest. What tools will help your heart become more tender toward Him?

NINE

THE PUTTY KNIFE

The putty knife has a flat blade that spreads putty like smooth peanut butter from a jar. An inexpensive tool, it is useful for a variety of projects. A builder often uses it to put wood filler into holes or hairline cracks or to scrape away old wallpaper. The putty knife is very forgiving. In a careful hand, this device quickly hides small errors and blemishes so they can be covered over and corrected. We all need that kind of mercy. So do those around us.

Salvation is when God uses His putty knife
of grace to cover our imperfections.

—*Michelle Cox*

Revealing What's Beneath

Look closely. Every wall in your house is flawed. If you don't see those imperfections, it's because someone worked magic with a putty knife. As the name suggests, the knife's purpose is to apply putty or joint compound to seams and to hide imperfections. Other important uses include spreading plaster and scraping off wallpaper, paint, stickers, or gunky glue. Typically the putty knife has a wide and flexible blade. The handle is usually short for easy control.

When it comes to the putty knife, the type of grip matters. A flexible handle is perfect for applying pliable materials. By contrast, a stiff handle is excellent for scraping unwanted surface coverings. However, beware, as the handle can bend and break under great pressure. The same admonition applies to the blade.

To remove an unwanted mess, you'll want a blade of rigid metal or hard plastic. For applying drywall mud or tape, the best choice is a flexible putty blade. The width and size of the blade is also important. A tiny half-inch blade will let you work with greater detail but will, of course, take more time. A wider blade is better for handling larger surfaces faster, especially when it's necessary to strip paint from a broad wall space.

Think of the contrasts between the tool used and the job that must be done. If you're doing some minor demolition, like scraping off a thin layer of paint or some other unsightly gummy substance, you want the biggest tool you can find for the job. Small jobs require more delicate tools.

Guess how God sees us? Most likely as a huge project with lots of work still to be done. He knows us at a heart level and realizes it's not enough to gently scratch away at our imperfections. For some of us, He needed the big putty knife to remove years of sticky sin and festering habits. Such scraping will be felt to the core. But it must be done for the remodeling to succeed. The old must make way for the new.

Once we've accepted Christ we may (foolishly) feel we don't need help anymore. We assume we're on track and don't need God hassling us about the fine details. Clearly, this would be the wrong way to look at a walk of faith. Instead of believing the lie that we have the strength to save ourselves by our own efforts, we must continually seek the Master's guiding hand.

Let's ask Him to keep using His smaller blade to smooth out the bumpy details that lessen our impact for Christ. God will forgive our spiritual imperfections, but we must submit to His detailed work and loving care. No matter how long it takes.

Seest thou a man diligent in his business?
He shall stand before kings; he shall not
stand before mean men.
—*Proverbs 22:29*

Lord, that shiny veneer is something the world throws in our faces all the time. Please show me that it's not the surface that matters. Truly. That's a tough message to internalize when the shallowest characters imaginable make headlines every day. Give me the courage to fill in the many little cracks and spaces in my soul with your hope, purity, and kindness. I need that putty knife to get to the things that I ignore. Let me whisper my little secrets to you, trusting that you will make me whole again, clean again. I'm your remodeling project. Do what you want with me. Thank you for seeing me as your forgiven man no matter what I may look like on the outside. Amen.

THE BUILDING PERMIT PAGE

WHAT WILL I PERMIT GOD TO DO IN MY LIFE?

1. Do you usually get down to the details when it comes to spiritual remodeling? Or do you try to overlook your shortcomings?

2. Are you that forgiving when it comes to over-looking weaknesses in other people? What can you do to help plug holes in the hearts of people who need God's love and kindness?

3. Sometimes it can take a lot of putty knife work to remove old wallpaper—but it always looks so fresh and clean afterward when the walls sport a new coat of paint. Think back to something God's removed from your life. How did that change you?

4. If you see yourself as God's home improvement project, what areas does He most need to work on? Make a list and ask Him to do a major rehab on you.

TEN

THE CHISEL

The chisel is a tool that removes material in a controlled way. It can be used on wood, metal, or stone. The chisel has a long blade with a shaped edge and can be pushed by hand into the wood or metal, or if more force is needed, a hammer or mallet can be used. Wood carvers generally start with larger chisels and work down to smaller ones for detail work.

You can't change circumstances
and you can't change other people,
but God can change you.
—*Evelyn A. Thiessen*

Looking Like Him

Many years ago, a preacher was driving through the winding twists and turns of a road in the Great Smoky Mountains en route to a speaking engagement. As he drove around a curve, he noticed a roadside stand with large carved wood figures on display. Even from a distance, he was amazed at the realistic detail of each piece.

He'd been driving for quite some time, so this provided a great opportunity to get out of the car and stretch for a bit. He pulled into the parking lot, shook off the stiffness as he got out of his car, and approached the figures for a closer look.

What he saw stunned him. The carving of a dog was so realistic that he almost expected to hear the dog bark at any minute. He moved on to the next piece and shook his head in awe at the lifelike carving of a bear. There was a raccoon in a playful pose. It looked like it would scamper into the woods at any moment. Next to that was a majestic eagle, wings raised outward as if it would take flight any second. Large logs were piled at the side of the roadside shop, waiting their turn to be touched by the master's hand.

Other travelers had gathered to watch the wood carver at work. The preacher joined them, and they watched in wonder as the carver picked up a piece of wood, took a tool into his hand, and started carving. Wood chips flew through the air, and soon the floppy ears and soulful eyes of a dog took form.

The preacher couldn't contain himself any longer, and he broke the silence. "How do you *do* that? How do you take a piece of inanimate hardwood and know how to make a dog?"

The carver shrugged, halted his chisel, and in a manner reminiscent of Michelangelo, he replied in a soft mountain drawl, "I just cut away anything that doesn't look like a dog."

As the wood carver cuts away the pieces of wood that shouldn't be there, God's controlling hand wants to take our hard hearts and chisel away anything that doesn't look like Him. When God looks at us, He doesn't just see what we are now; He sees what we can become if we let Him have His way in our lives.

What are you holding on to in your life? Is it pride? Looking at pornography? A refusal to give up control? A hard heart? Allow God to chip away everything that shouldn't be there. The process might be painful for a while, but it will be worth it when the Master Carver can put you on display as one of His best, most amazing creations.

So God created man in his own image,
in the image of God created he him.
—*Genesis 1:27*

Lord, I know you must be frustrated sometimes by my hard heart when you want to make changes in me. Make me tender toward you. Show me the things in my life that you need to cut away so I can be closer to you, so I can become the man of God you desire me to be. I realize some of those changes might be painful or require sacrifice. Give me a willing heart to accept the necessary changes. Help me to live my life in a manner that allows others to see you when they look at me—especially my family. Amen.

THE BUILDING PERMIT PAGE

WHAT WILL I PERMIT GOD TO DO IN MY LIFE?

1. The detail of the carver's pieces amazed those who saw them. How did he achieve that, and how does that apply to us spiritually?

2. All of us have things in our lives that keep us from becoming fully committed men of God. What does God need to chisel away in your life to make you more like Him?

3. Sometimes it's easy to recognize what needs to change in our hearts, but it's difficult to make those changes. Are you willing for the Master Carver to begin working on you? What steps do you need to take to get started?

4. The carver used tools to work on the logs. Our tools are God's Word and time spent with Him. Are you spending enough time reading your Bible and in prayer?

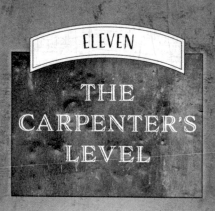

ELEVEN

THE CARPENTER'S LEVEL

The level is an instrument used to determine if a surface is aligned with the horizon. This vital tool uses bubble vials, typically in the center and at both ends, to make sure that the vertical and horizontal surfaces are level. Usually about two feet in length, the carpenter's level is constructed of hardwood with metal bindings or shatterproof plastic. Masons' levels are up to six feet in length. Such tools are useful for building, hanging pictures, and installing level shelves.

The only way a man can stay on
the straight and level for God is to
build a firm foundation of faith.
—Michelle Cox

STAYING STEADY

A level is a vital tool because it keeps us connected to the ideal, to the way things are supposed to be done. You know what I mean. Some of us can hang a picture without pulling out a level. It looks good enough to our eyes—at least until our better half insists we need to hang her artwork the right way. And that's where the level comes in.

When you build a foundation without keeping things level, your small mistake becomes obvious as the walls are raised. In fact, if you don't consult your small sturdy level when building an addition to the house, installing shelves, or even hanging a door, the lack shows. And not in a good way.

Without a level, molding doesn't match. Windows don't shut. Toilets totter. We've all been there. Either we've been rushed to finish a job (so we can watch the big game), or we just decide we're not going to bother. We take a shortcut, the easy way, and get nothing but trouble.

As Christians, we squirm at questions about whether or not we're "on the level." Sure we are … sometimes. But all the time? Probably not. It's easier to try our best and hope for decent results. We pitifully plead, "I can't be careful all the time." Sometimes we veer a little to one side or the other. That's just the way guys are.

Maybe, but that's no excuse. It's like dabbling in a little

bit of sin, doing something sorta shady on the side, barely missing the mark. Or saying it's all right to take a small, controlled step into the darkness. We're strong enough to do that because we know the difference between right and wrong. And we can come back to the straight and level whenever we want. Sure we can. We all have our favorite justifications. But they're not going to keep us steady and ready to do our best.

Keep in mind that we don't live life alone. There are lots of little and big eyes watching—like our own children or grandchildren, or the neighbor kids, or our boss and coworkers. When we stop putting first things first, others notice that our foundation is shaky—because they're impacted too. And often those within our realm of influence start justifying themselves, ignoring the baseline, and slipping off level ground as well.

You're a bigger man than that. Don't give others that easy out. And don't try to latch on to that phony excuse for yourself. Keep life level by reading His Word and spending time in prayer. You'll never regret building a firm foundation with God.

For other foundation can no man lay than
that is laid, which is Jesus Christ.
—*1 Corinthians 3:11*

Father, you know what the terrain is like out there. When you walked the dusty roads of Nazareth, there was very little level ground. And your accusers certainly didn't care a whit about keeping the playing field level. As I walk along the slippery slopes of an ever-darkening culture, I am constantly challenged to keep my feet on the right path. I know that a small crack in the foundation of my life can cause imbalances that make me totter and tip. Help me to fix problems as they appear. Show me how to be more like you—more firm in my beliefs, more assured of my service to you and my family. As much as it hurts at times, thanks for keeping me on the level, Lord. Amen.

THE BUILDING PERMIT PAGE

WHAT WILL I PERMIT GOD TO DO IN MY LIFE?

1. Taking home repair shortcuts can cause problems. The same is true spiritually. What shortcuts have you taken? What were the repercussions?

2. You may have a carpenter's level, but what other kinds of levels do you need in your life? Are you active in a men's group or Bible study that requires you to remain accountable to others for the things that are done in secret? In what ways do you come alongside others to bring them hope and encouragement?

3. When do you find yourself most susceptible to temptation? How do you recognize you're slipping off the path—and what helps you to regain your footing?

4. What responsibilities do you have as a father, husband, and friend to help and encourage others to stay on the path of righteousness? How do you accomplish this?

TWELVE

THE FIRST AID KIT

A first aid kit is a box filled with medical supplies such as bandages, alcohol wipes, tweezers, and burn cream. Folks who use tools will usually have one readily available in their toolboxes, and a wise builder will keep that kit well-stocked, replacing items as they run low. A bright red cross is found on the top of most first aid kits, making them easily recognizable to anyone who is looking for them when a crisis happens. Emergencies occur at moments when we least expect them, so it's a good idea to always be prepared.

Whenever those emergencies of life slam
into you, you'll find that God's first aid kit
is stocked with all that you need.
—Michelle Cox

Just Look for the Cross

First aid kits often get called into use when guys are working with their tools. Admit it, we're accidents waiting to happen. We sport bruises from where our buddies weren't careful enough with where they placed the two-by-fours ... and we walked into them. Yeah, the aspirin from the first aid kit was much appreciated that day. And the bandages—even though they were Hello Kitty ones.

We have swollen black-and-blue thumbs from where we didn't get them out of the way while swinging a hammer. And we have cuts and scrapes from where we carelessly handled sharp metal or rusty nails.

But, hey, we're guys. Those bumps, scrapes, and bruises give us something to talk about with our buddies. We won't admit it to our pals, but sometimes those injuries *hurt*. It's amazing how those pounded-with-a-hammer thumb injuries can keep a man up all night while they throb with every heartbeat.

And while we won't admit it most of the time (because we *are* macho men), there are times in our lives when we are hurting. Moments that slam into us like that day we encountered the two-by-four.

Sometimes our hearts are aching from family problems or the loss of a job—deep aches that no medicine from the first aid kit can cure. Other times it can be discouragement as our dreams are shattered or as we're struggling to make ends meet. And often we bottle those things inside, allowing them to build up until we have an emergency emotional situation where we snap at our loved ones out of frustration or we break down completely.

That's where discovering the first aid kit in God's toolbox can offer so much relief. His also comes with a recognizable cross so that we can find it easily in emergency situations. Those precious promises in His Word are like a salve to our souls. They can reach into the dark places of our hearts, providing bandages placed by a nail-scarred hand.

And just as many of our injury situations on the jobsite can be avoided by reading the warnings on our tools, we can often avoid injuring ourselves and our families if we'll read—and pay attention to—God's warnings for us.

A builder doesn't ever want his jobsite to come to a screeching halt due to an accident or injury, but by reaching into the first aid kit for bandages, antiseptic wipes, or pain medicines, his workers will often be able to make it through the rest of the day.

So whenever you're having one of those battered-and-bruised moments, find God's first aid kit and pull out some mercy and grace. Keep your spiritual first aid kit well-stocked so you can find it whenever those emergencies of life come your way—and then, just look for the cross.

He healeth the broken in heart,
and bindeth up their wounds.
—*Psalm 147:3*

Lord, I might not admit it very often, but there are times when I'm battered and bruised from heartache, regrets, or fear. Just as a builder stocks a first aid kit for unexpected emergency moments on the worksite, remind me to come to you when I'm wounded and when I need comfort. Sometimes those injuries in my life happen because of my foolishness or disobedience. Don't let me forget that my actions can also wound those I love. Help me to heed your warnings. Lead me to the cross, keep me close to your first aid kit of mercy and grace, and build me into a man who is whole and strong for you. Amen.

THE BUILDING PERMIT PAGE

WHAT WILL I PERMIT GOD TO DO IN MY LIFE?

1. Sometimes we do stupid stuff as we're working on building projects, and we do the same in our spiritual lives. We fail to heed the warnings. How does that apply to us spiritually as well as physically, and what can we do to avoid that in the future?

2. Many of us come to God as battered and bruised souls. Think of times when God's bandaged your heart. What did you learn from those situations?

3. Most first aid kits come with a red cross on the box so folks can find them easily. Why do we forget to go straight to the cross when we're hurting spiritually or emotionally?

4. Emergencies can happen when we're working with tools, but they can also happen in our lives. What can you do to be prepared for those moments?

THIRTEEN

THE STRING

String is a flexible cord usually made of fiber used for fastening, tying, or lacing. When a contractor starts a foundation for a house, he uses an instrument to determine where the footings are supposed to go. He then hammers pieces of wood into the ground and attaches string to each corner to show the layout of the house. This helps the builder visualize how the project will ultimately look. But if he doesn't have a plan—and follow it carefully—the entire building project is in jeopardy.

Grace binds you with far stronger cords
than the cords of duty or obligation can bind you.
Grace is free, but when once you take it,
you are bound forever to the Giver.
—E. Stanley Jones

TYING IT ALL TOGETHER

You can think of string as prehistoric duct tape. Once upon a time, every respectable work bench had a big ball of twine. Small towns discovered a claim to fame for having the largest ball of string. Families drove for miles to take pictures and be astonished.

Around the house and shop, string was (and is) used for everything from tying up bundles of branch cuttings for trash removal to popping a chalk-string line to make sure that molding, shingles, or wallpaper are straight. Of course, string also still serves the purpose of a memory jogger tied around a finger. Who can forget that? (Although our wives might comment that there's not enough string in the world to make us remember things.)

One reason string is such a popular tool is because it's cheap and expendable. It's a throw-away item. Tossed in the trash without thought or regret.

It's used to mark out a new concrete driveway or sidewalk. Or as a needed guide for laying brick or a foundation—a vital necessity for the house to have straight lines. It can bind pieces of a wooden chair or favorite toy that have been painstakingly glued together. But after the project is complete, the string is no longer needed. Into the garbage it goes.

How is the Savior like string? String is nothing beautiful

to look at and not considered worthy of esteem and admiration. It has no inherent value and to the casual observer has no lasting worth. It is just cheap string. Used in great quantities and cut to pieces without any compunction or thought.

The world at large saw the Savior that same way. Jesus Christ was bound tightly to a rough cross of wood. He was not viewed as valuable, worthwhile, or needed. Few wept at the death of this man who loved sinners. Without any compunction, they threw away His offer of hope and salvation. And yet this Jesus, born a helpless babe to a poor family, was the Son of God. He rose exultant from the dead, surprising the world, especially those who mocked and hated Him.

Like woven string, He created a connection that drew us to God the Father—and His great love held together our battered and broken hearts. So the next time you toss aside a measure of string, contemplate how God used His simple string of mercy and grace to tie us to Him for eternity.

Sometimes the smallest, most insignificant tool in the toolbox is really the most needed and ultimately the most valuable. When we're tied closely to Him, we can be exactly who God requires to fulfill His wide-ranging and amazing purposes, His sometimes tiny but always mighty goals.

Draw nigh to God,
and he will draw nigh to you.
—James 4:8

Oh God, thank you for being so intimately entangled in my life. Sometimes I think I have measured everything out perfectly, and then something sets me off—a phone call, a news story, an unexpected bill. I realize once again that I don't have it all under control. I know that I need you. When I start living life as if I am the master of my own journey, I can rest assured that a fall is coming. Another mistake, more problems. You are like gentle string wrapped around the broken and bent pieces of my heart. You bind them together with loving strength so I barely feel the pain. And when I heal, all that remains are the imprints of your love. Tie me close to you, Lord. Amen.

THE BUILDING PERMIT PAGE

WHAT WILL I PERMIT GOD TO DO IN MY LIFE?

1. String can become a mess when it gets tangled. Our lives are often tangled messes as well. What can you do to keep that from happening spiritually?

2. What kind of security does it give you to know that God has you firmly tied to Him? How could you share that message with someone else?

3. The builder uses string to mark the lines for a new house so everything will be straight. What can you do to make sure everything in your spiritual life is in line with what God wants from you?

4. Used string is usually thrown away. Many people have also thrown away the gift of salvation that God offers to us. Have you accepted that offer? How has your life changed as a result?

FOURTEEN

THE NAILS

Nails are fastening devices used in the carpentry field. Nails sit in a box, labeled, until time for the right project. While using plenty of nails during construction is important, removing those nails at a later date can be boring and time-consuming—as many a man can attest after spending hours (or days) pulling them out one at a time. There's truly no such thing as instant results. But demolition work is necessary before we can move ahead with the job.

Nail down your commitment to God—
and avoid a lengthy demo process before
He can make something special out of you.

—*Michelle Cox*

SOUL REMODELING

Mike sighed as he looked out the window at the gorgeous spring day. It was a golf course kind of afternoon, but he was stuck at home accomplishing another item on his wife's "honey-do" list.

Yeah, it was one of the things he'd promised to do when they purchased their home five years ago. As any guy knows, that's really super quick for us to get around to things.

Don't get Mike wrong. He loves making his wife happy. It's just that this task had turned into a monster of a boring, hard-on-the-knees-and-back job.

Ripping up the old carpet had been easy. Demo and mess making is always fun. But then Mike discovered that when the installer had nailed the carpet padding down, he'd taken no chances that it would ever come up. Ever.

It didn't take long for Mike to realize he had *thousands* of nails to remove. After several hours, he could have sworn somebody was coming behind him adding new ones, because it didn't look like he was making any progress. What was supposed to be a Saturday project ended up taking days to complete. Several *long* days.

But once the floor was cleaned and he'd added a coat of polyurethane, that wood gleamed, much like Mike's wife's face when she saw the finished project. And that made the crick in his neck and the aches in his back worth every minute of it.

It's the same with our spiritual lives. Just as Mike had to get rid of the nails that didn't belong in the hardwood floor, we have things that we need to remove from our lives. Soul demo usually isn't a fun process as pet sins come to life, but when God convicts our hearts about them, they must go.

Maybe it's the magazines we've been looking at when nobody is around. Or it might be the sites we've visited on the Internet, with images that can creep in and destroy our relationships and homes.

Or maybe it's that we haven't touched our Bibles in weeks or prayed for our loved ones. Or we've slacked off about attending church with our families, spending Sunday mornings feeding our lawns instead of feeding our faith.

We must decide if we truly want our lives to be usable for God and an example for our children. We need to steadily remove the things that will damage our relationship with Him—and then as He coats our souls with the polyurethane of His grace, we can become men whose lives will gleam for Him.

The nails in the floor would have damaged people's feet if Mike hadn't removed them—and the known sins in our lives can damage our testimonies and those we love if we leave them there.

Search me, O God, and know my heart:
try me, and know my thoughts: And see if
there be any wicked way in me,
and lead me in the way everlasting.
—*Psalm 139:23–24*

Father, ripping out walls and cabinets in a house can be fun, whereas soul demo—ripping out the things in my heart that shouldn't be there—is often painful. But I realize it's necessary. Search me, God. Convict my heart about things that are keeping me from a full relationship with you. Make me tender toward you, and help me to be still long enough to hear what you want to tell me. I want to be a man after your heart. I want to make you proud. I don't ever want to damage my family or others by the way that I live each day, so polish me with your mercy and grace so I'll gleam for you. Amen.

THE BUILDING PERMIT PAGE

WHAT WILL I PERMIT GOD TO DO IN MY LIFE?

1. Remodeling demo often seems like fun when we start, but it can quickly lose its appeal. Soul demo is the same. What do you need to remodel spiritually?

2. Removing old nails from a piece of wood can be uncomfortable. Removing old sins can also be painful. Why do you think it hurts so much to turn loose of the things God asks us to remove from our lives?

3. Turning the yucky carpeted floors into beautiful hardwood made Mike's wife happy. How do you think it impacts God when He sees us removing the messed-up things in our lives so that we can shine for Him?

4. What are three things you can do to become the man God wants you to be?

FIFTEEN

THE WRENCH

A wrench gives a man a real bite on a problem. With fixed or adjustable jaws, the wrench grabs hold of a tight rusty nut, for example, and provides a grip to turn and twist. There are specialty wrenches for engines, bikes, and pretty much anything you might need to work on. As for leaky pipes, a plumber often gives a sudden forcible rotation at just the right moment ... or sometimes at just the wrong moment when working on old plumbing.

When disaster strikes, dial up God's emergency number. He's available 24/7.

—John Perrodin

WORKING LIKE A PRO

Johnny is an experienced professional but admittedly a novice plumber. He's got a new pipe wrench, though, and he knows there's a leak making a mess under his daughter's bathroom sink. He's got to fix it now. Or call a plumber.

No way is he going to hire someone to do a job he's perfectly capable of. With his phone, he's got the wisdom of the ages at his fingertips—videos, articles, and discussion forums. What could go wrong?

As he reaches to turn off the water supply to the sink, the rusty faucet won't turn. Johnny's brute force causes it to bubble, then spray. Great. A new problem. Muttering, Johnny heads for the water main, shouts a warning on the way down the stairs, and switches the flow off for the whole house.

Upside down, cramped, and uncomfortable, he's finally in position to fix things. As Johnny yanks on the pipe with his tightly clamped wrench, it gives way completely. Immediately a glob of black gunk smacks his nose and mouth. He comes up sputtering and spitting. In loosening one pipe, he accidentally pushed another out of place. Plus, he notices a new crack that he caused by exerting too much pressure.

He sees a cautious smile above him. "Maybe you should call a plumber," his wife offers helpfully.

The man knows he's beat. He speaks into his phone.

"Plumbing emergency," he tells the robotic female voice. Wiping the black crud on an embroidered guest towel, he says, "Dial."

How many of us men have started a project and then realized we were in way over our heads? Maybe even treading water when our plumbing projects go awry. Dealing with explosive frustration affects us physically and spiritually. Yes, we forget about those past prayers to keep things in perspective. And what happened to the resolutions to de-stress and ask for help when we need it?

Sometimes we need to call the professional. Sure, there are costs involved that we need to count, but there may be no other option if we want the job done right. We've all seen examples of the shoddy work done by the previous owner of the house.

When it comes to our spiritual life, God is no amateur. We've got to ask for help when we need it. Nothing is gained by pretending we have it all under control. Especially when the frustration is clearly showing. We're not fooling God. In fact, the longer we wait, the worse the situation becomes.

Maybe before we start the next "quick-fix" effort in the bathroom, we should put the wrench down and get on our knees to ask for God's guidance. No matter what your plan, give in and go to God first. Dial Him up on your prayer line. He's available 24/7.

A wise man is strong;
yea, a man of knowledge increaseth strength.
—*Proverbs 24:5*

Dear Lord, when I look in the mirror, I see Mr. Spontaneous has disappeared. With all my work and family responsibilities, I don't have the freedom I used to. And that's okay. In exchange for the constant fluidity of a young man's schedule, I now have things that matter more. Much more. And yet that also means I get my wheels stuck in ruts. I expect things to be done a certain way—all the time—without fail. I want people to read my mind, which my kids and coworkers and my beloved don't always appreciate. Take your wrench to me, God. Loosen me up so I can hear your Spirit calling, pray more, and help others whenever they have needs. Make me yours, Lord. And remind me that I'll deal with fewer messes if I'll remember to dial you up first for guidance. Amen.

THE BUILDING PERMIT PAGE

WHAT WILL I PERMIT GOD TO DO IN MY LIFE?

1. What's the one area—physically and spiritually—where you have the most difficulty accepting guidance?

2. Sometimes God sends unexpected moments into our lives for which we are not prepared. How do you respond to those situations? With anger or bitterness? Have you learned to let God's loving presence flow as naturally as water from a working faucet?

3. If you were being completely objective and honest, are you an easy person to live with, or are you the equivalent of the yucky gunk that Johnny encountered in his plumbing project? List some ways you could improve.

4. If God needed you to change dramatically, what kind of wrench (pressure) would He need to use to get your attention?

FOURTEEN

THE PRY BAR (CROWBAR)

Having a somewhat notorious history, a jimmy bar was often used by burglars to pry open windows and make off with the occupants' possessions. Nowadays, however, the renamed pry bar, or crowbar, has been rehabilitated and serves many valuable purposes. It comes in especially handy when something old and broken down needs to be removed and restored. A crowbar works well for opening up wooden shipping crates. It can also provide leverage for heavy objects and poke its "nose" into small spaces.

The crowbar of Christ strips off burdens that make our hearts hard and resistant to correction.

—*John Perrodin*

PRYING AWAY BARRIERS

The pry bar is a powerful instrument of destruction. This removal tool wasn't designed to build and create but rather to pull down, tear away, and set the stage for something new and better.

When we reflect on its helpful uses, what comes to mind are things such as removing nails embedded in wood or ripping out a rusted screw. This handy bar is also perfect for stripping away dented baseboards or tearing apart facades that once looked grand but are now only grungy. If you add the impact of a hammer, the pry bar can lift tile from countertops, bathrooms, and floors.

We have so many ambitious plans for creative projects that would allow us to use our imaginations. But before we know it, we're facing more "honey-dos" than our lists can hold. What we want—what we need—is a fresh start.

Wouldn't it be great to stop digging yourself out and start moving ahead? What a dream come true to create fun toys we've imagined, build fancy play equipment, or fashion miniature furniture for a homemade dollhouse. We'd be heroes to the children and grandchildren. But how do we climb out from under the mounds that bury us?

When it comes to demolishing the status quo, the pry bar is a mighty valuable tool. You may or may not need one to pry up old tiles or baseboards, but do start some-where. Making a little progress is always better than doing nothing.

Now visualize hefting your spiritual pry bar. It comes with a notch at the end for yanking out rusty old attitudes and popping out habits that have pinned us in place for years. Our faithful pry bar leverages off old distractions and demolishes pointless worries.

We often ignore the fact that our body, mind, and spirit need to rest and relax. A soul needs to dwell on Scripture to remain whole. With all of the demands we place on ourselves, we can't hope to accomplish everything on our punch lists, let alone anything extra. Sometimes only a spiritual pry bar will work to remove the load from us.

Often, burdens have been building up for years. They will need to be disassembled board by board. Thankfully, the Word of God can break down fears. And steadfast prayer can knock down mountains of worry if we are diligent to petition the Father.

We all need hope for the future. But unless we clear out the stuff that sits on the sidelines waiting to trip us up, we'll always feel stuck.

Spiritual pry bars can yank off facades we've put up to show ourselves as something we're not, and the crowbar of Christ can strip off burdens that make our hearts hard and resistant to correction.

Yeah, we're men, but it's okay to say, "I don't know how to fix things." We don't have the strength to change ourselves. Only the power of the Holy Spirit can pry us free.

For my yoke is easy,
and my burden is light.
—Matthew 11:30

Lord, when I'm doing my clam imitation, help me to see how I'm only hurting myself and my relationships with others. If I'm honest with myself, I realize that many times I need someone—usually my sweetheart—to pry me open. Communication shouldn't be so difficult. Give me opportunities to share my thoughts and feelings, first with you, and then with those I love. I admit I'm overscheduled. And overtired and overcommitted. Show me how to pry off the burdensome layers and get down to the work I am responsible for. Teach me to better delegate and to make more time to recharge with your Word. I know I need you. Thanks for hearing my prayers and always answering. Amen.

THE BUILDING PERMIT PAGE

WHAT WILL I PERMIT GOD TO DO IN MY LIFE?

1. Have you ever undertaken a remodeling project? What about remodeling your heart and attitude? How will both of those situations affect your relationships?

2. How do you want others (boss, coworkers, neighbors, family, and friends) to see you—and is the picture you present the real you or just a facade?

3. What are some of the "extras" that you need to cut back on? Why do you have difficulty firmly saying no when someone asks you to take on new tasks? How can you better protect yourself and your time?

4. It's not fun feeling as if your life is out of control. How did things get that way? Take time to pray and ask God to be the keeper of your schedule.

SEVENTEEN

THE DUCT TAPE

Duct tape is a wide adhesive tape originally designed to secure ductwork for furnaces. Homeowners sometimes use it on glass windows when hurricane warnings are in effect. Duct tape is some awesome stuff! It is useful for almost anything that needs a quick repair—and folks have been known to use it for some amazingly creative things. Some men consider it their must-have item when it comes to home repairs. It goes on smoothly, has great holding power, and is water resistant—but it's not meant for permanent repairs.

A spiritual heart cannot be repaired with duct tape or unused tools. Wipe the dust off your Bible and make some permanent repairs.
—Michelle Cox

Dusty Tools

Albert considered duct tape one of his best friends, especially when it came to making home repairs. He'd used it for so many crazy things that his buddies teased him that he could solve the problems of the world with it. They'd ribbed him unmercifully when he helped his daughter make a dress out of duct tape to wear to a school function—but they'd been amazed at the odd beauty of the garment.

Albert had used duct tape to make repairs for many years. When the plumbing sprang a leak under the sink, Albert wrapped thick layers of duct tape around the pipe.

When a tile in the bathroom came loose, Albert rolled duct tape around his hand so it would be sticky on both sides, and then he put it under the tile. Voilà! Instant fix.

When the piece holding the garage door rollers fell off, Albert stuck it back on with—you guessed it—duct tape.

The same was true of the door that covered the furnace filter. Mr. Duct Tape Repairman fixed it with his trusty roll of tape. It was the magic cure-all!

But then as months and years went by, Albert had to face an uncomfortable reality. If he'd just picked up his tools and used them to do the job right the first time, he wouldn't have had such expensive problems to deal with later.

You see, that leaky pipe he thought he'd fixed had still

been leaking tiny but steady drops that rotted the floor and the bottom of the cabinets. The loose tile he'd "repaired" had kept shifting, loosening up adjacent tiles, causing several of them to break.

The "fix" on the furnace filter had allowed dirt and dust to accumulate there, clogging the furnace and requiring an expensive repair.

And let's just say Albert's wife wasn't too happy with him when the roller to the garage door popped off, hit her on the head, and sent her for an unexpected vacation at the hospital.

You know what's sad? Albert had a toolbox full of expensive tools, but he never used them. They just sat there, collecting dust so thick that he couldn't even determine the color of the toolbox.

Guys, what about us? Are we guilty of having unused tools spiritually? Are our Bibles gathering dust because we haven't read them? Is our prayer life rusty because it hasn't been used? Are we breaking relationships because we've used the equivalent of a duct tape patch instead of fixing the issues that are rotting our souls?

Let's not be guilty of having dusty spiritual tools. They were expensive, paid for by the sacrifice of the God who loved us so much that He died for us—and He means for us to put them to good use so that our homes and hearts are well-maintained spiritually.

Study to shew thyself approved unto God,
a workman that needeth not to be ashamed,
rightly dividing the word of truth.
—*2 Timothy 2:15*

Lord, sometimes there are issues in my heart, and instead of asking you to forgive me and to fix those flaws in my soul, I put the equivalent of duct tape on them, making a temporary repair. But that doesn't take care of the deeper issue. God, I don't want problems to arise down the road for my family because I refused to surrender to whatever you placed on my heart. You've supplied the tools I need to know how to be a man after your heart, but I realize they don't do me any good unless I use them. Help me to wipe the dust off my Bible and the dust off my heart. Build me into what you want me to be. Amen.

THE BUILDING PERMIT PAGE

WHAT WILL I PERMIT GOD TO DO IN MY LIFE?

1. Instead of fixing things the right way, Albert made some temporary repairs—and it cost him. How does it affect us spiritually when we don't do necessary repairs for our soul?

2. By using duct tape on the furnace door, it allowed dirt and grime to get in and clog the furnace. What happens when we allow the dirt and grime of life into our hearts?

3. Albert's wife was injured when the duct tape patch on the garage door allowed the roller to pop loose. How does it injure those we love when we neglect ourselves spiritually?

4. Are you guilty of having unused or dusty tools? If so, spend some time with God today and determine to become a workman who won't be ashamed of his faith.

EIGHTEEN

THE SANDPAPER

Sandpaper is paper coated with an abrasive material on one side. The carpenter takes a piece of sandpaper and begins by roughing up the surface of a piece of furniture to remove ugly stains and impurities. The abrasive coating on sandpaper can become worn after use, and the carpenter then uses a new piece to continue the process. And then with a steady hand, he uses progressively finer pieces of sandpaper until he has removed all surface scratches and blemishes. The result is a piece of quality furniture ready for use.

Forgiveness does not change the past,
but it does enlarge the future.
—*Paul Boese*

SANDING THE GUILT AWAY

Jim was a master carpenter. His talent was handed down by his father and grandfather, a gift given to him by God. Jim could take a piece of wood and turn it into a work of art. Wealthy customers clamored for his time, begging him to build the cabinetry in their million-dollar homes, and the price didn't matter to them.

Jim's work appeared flawless when he was finished. Part of that came from the hours that he spent sanding the pieces. First, he roughed up the surface to get rid of impurities in the wood, then he used progressively finer pieces of sandpaper, removing splinters and sanding away imperfections until the texture was smooth.

His carpentry business was booming, but Jim couldn't say the same about his personal life. It was a mess, and he couldn't get over the guilt of his past. His addiction to alcohol had destroyed his family. They'd lost their house because he'd spent all the money on booze. The memories of his wife's black eyes and broken arms and the terrified expressions on his children's faces were horror-show images that played repeatedly in his mind. Life was a mess of his own making.

Then he met Jesus—the turning point in Jim's life as a nail-scarred hand lovingly sanded away the impurities,

smoothing out the surface of Jim's heart until it was a thing of true beauty.

Jim had gone to rehab. It had been rough, but he'd been sober for ten years now. Miraculously, when they saw the changed man he'd become, his wife and children forgave him. It took several years to patch their family back together, but their home had been a different place—one where his children and wife were happy, where they went to bed at night without fear.

But Jim couldn't get over the guilt. It ate at him day and night. God had forgiven him, his family had forgiven him, but Jim couldn't forgive himself for what he'd done to those he loved.

And then one day as Jim worked in his shop, he heard a whisper from God in his soul. *Jim, what comments do folks make about your work? Do you hear, "Oh, look at that board!" when they see your handiwork? No, they look at the finished perfection and say, "Jim, what gorgeous cabinets!" and then they are glad to pay the price—even though it's high.*

As Jim continued sanding, smoothing away the splinters and rough places, God whispered again, *Jim, you're my project. I've sanded away your imperfections—the wrongs of your past—and have turned you into a beautiful finished product. I paid the price and was glad to do it.*

And then came the words that healed Jim's heart: *You're no longer what you were, my son. You're now my* new *creation.*

Therefore if any man be in Christ, he is a
new creature: old things are passed away;
behold, all things are become new.
—*2 Corinthians 5:17*

*Father, my rough spots and imperfections are so
obvious as I come to you. Thank you for lovingly
using your sandpaper of grace to shape me. So
many times I look back at where I've been and
what I've done (or not done) and the guilt eats into
my soul. Change me, Lord. Take this flawed heart
that longs to be like you and make me into a new
creation. Thank you for your forgiveness, for loving
me when I wasn't loveable. Thank you for paying
the price for me even though I didn't deserve it. I
love you, God. My heart is yours. Do what you want
with it. Amen.*

THE BUILDING PERMIT PAGE

WHAT WILL I PERMIT GOD TO DO IN MY LIFE?

1. Jim used sandpaper to remove imperfections and rough places from the wood he used for his custom cabinetry. How can we apply that spiritually?

2. God uses His sandpaper of grace to smooth out the rough places in us. Sometimes that can be painful. What has God fixed in your life? Take a look back at where you were and what He's done for you and then thank Him.

3. His family and God forgave Jim, but he couldn't forgive himself. He couldn't get over the guilt. Have you ever experienced that? What helped you get past it?

4. We all have things in our past that we'd like to forget, but none of it goes to waste. What have you learned from your past that you could use to help someone else?

NINETEEN

THE SAFETY GLASSES

Our sight is a precious gift. So it's vital that we take steps to safeguard our vision. Safety glasses or goggles provide eye protection for projects large and small. They help prevent eye injury or permanent loss of sight due to carelessness or wayward pieces of wood or metal. When you think you'll be fine *without* your goggles, a flashing red warning light should go off in your head. Put them on and be safe instead.

Spiritual safety glasses will protect
your eyes from the distractions of this world.

—Michelle Cox

CARING FOR YOUR EYES

We've all laughed about those warnings and disclaimers that go beyond protecting us to treating us like children. One area, however, where full attention is always warranted would be safety warnings about our eyes. God gave us only one special pair, and we owe it to ourselves, our families, and our livelihoods to protect them.

Some of the most dangerous aspects of using tools from our toolboxes are the little flying bits and pieces that are nearly invisible to the naked eye. Those mini projectiles move too fast for anyone to react to and avoid them. Even mowing the lawn or using a weed trimmer can kick up debris that can tear into sensitive tissue.

God had the great idea of giving us lashes and lids to provide some protection, but that may not be enough. Typically we close our eyes too late, *after* we feel the sharp pain. Even a tiny cut can be excruciating and cause long-lasting damage.

That's where the safety glasses come in. They're available in all shapes, sizes, and prices, and you can even get a prescription version if you'd like. Some styles are made to fit over your regular eyeglasses. Remember, they won't do any good stuffed in your toolbox or stowed behind the seat of your truck. Whenever there's the chance for spinning or tearing items to spit into your face, slap on those goggles.

Life likes to throw distractions at us that will keep us off track from the good things God has for us. Instead of reading God's Word, we sit in front of the TV. It's hard to focus on the best things—God, others, creation—because there are just so many tempting options these days. The competition for our eyeballs is enormous and comes in many forms.

Just as we need to cover our eyes in the shop, we need to pull down the visor on the helmet of salvation to protect our spiritual eyes. Otherwise we'll find that instead of seeing God's gift of hope, we become blinded by distractions. If we don't open our eyes to God's truth in Scripture, this weary world can blind us with hopelessness.

We need God to sharpen our focus and to help us avoid places that endanger our eyes—and our hearts. We can do harm to our very soul when we're not careful. If we look at things that take us far from Him, we may find the road home has disappeared from view. And once we get too far off the path, it becomes a fight to return.

It's simple: safety glasses protect your eyes when working in the shop, and your spiritual helmet visor protects you from encounters with the Dark One. With God's help, you will emerge into the light—with your eyes both wide open and protected.

The eyes of your understanding being
enlightened; that ye may know what
is the hope of his calling.
—*Ephesians 1:18*

*Oh God, I try to blame my tired eyes, but it's my
own weakness, my own temptation that prods me
to forgo what's good for me and partake in what's
merely enticing. If I look, I know all about what you
have given me. I see the gifts in my life, in my heart,
and in my home, and yet at times I feel tempted to
throw it all away because of something that catches
my eye. A shiny lure causes me to bobble the good
gifts I already hold in my hand. Protect me, Lord.
Please guard my eyesight and give me a vision to
follow you and you alone. I know you love me and
that I need only seek your goodness to be joy filled
and content. All I must do is ask. Amen.*

THE BUILDING PERMIT PAGE

WHAT WILL I PERMIT GOD TO DO IN MY LIFE?

1. What's the most dangerous thing about leaving your eyes unprotected? Consider both the physical and spiritual aspects of this question.

2. How should you respond when faced with temptations of the eyes (such as looking at women other than your wife, pornography, or movies with explicit content)? When you see others who are battling those temptations, what's the best way to help them?

3. Sometimes we close our eyes when God tries to show us things we need to correct in our lives. Why does that happen, and how can that be harmful?

4. Sight is such a precious gift. Spiritual insights are also special. What are some things God's shown you that have helped you become a better man?

TWENTY

THE NON-CONTACT VOLTAGE TESTER

Electricians use a voltage tester when working with electricity to locate breaks along live wires and to detect power prior to service. It detects the presence of AC voltage and then sends out both an audible signal and a bright LED indicator to alert them that voltage is present and that the situation could be dangerous. Failure to check for electricity can cause injuries and even death, so the non-contact voltage tester is an important tool for any builder or do-it-yourselfer.

* * *

A man who's wired into God
will avoid the jolts of life.
—Michelle Cox

HEED THE WARNINGS

Sparks shot across the room as Jim's screwdriver touched the raw wires. He was fortunate that he didn't get shocked worse. He wouldn't admit it to others, but that jolt of electricity had scared him. His wife had told him to hire an electrician, but Jim had been confident he could do the work himself.

An electrician friend from church had told Jim to get a non-contact voltage tester and warned him about working without it, but Jim hadn't wanted to spend the money. He didn't figure buying (or not buying) one was that big of a deal.

He'd also neglected to gain the knowledge he needed prior to starting the work. The warnings had been there in the instructions that came with the materials for the new light fixture, but he hadn't paid attention. One would have thought he'd learn his lesson from the shooting-sparks incident, but it didn't happen.

Then Jim made another mistake. He ignored the warning once again as he went ahead and installed the light and flipped the switch for the new fixture. Unlike the first episode with the sparks of electricity, the next incident had much graver implications. You see, that night while his family was sleeping, their house caught on fire ... from the wires that Jim had installed incorrectly.

They were grateful to make it out with their lives, but

Jim's wife received such bad injuries that she had to be air-lifted to the burn center. Her scars were daily reminders that Jim hadn't heeded the warnings.

For years, Jim has lived with the guilt of that mistake, wishing with all his heart that he could go back and do it over again. But no matter how much he wants to, he can't go back and rewind that day.

We shake our heads at Jim's foolishness, but don't we do the same things spiritually? God sends us warning after warning in His Word. With His equivalent of the non-contact voltage tester, God pinpoints danger areas. He tells us what to stay away from and what will harm us and our families—but we don't pay attention.

He gives us all the instructions we need for our lives, but we don't take the time to read them. Sometimes He even sends those shooting-sparks moments into our lives, warnings that if we continue on with what we're doing, there will be implications ahead.

Guys, don't keep on in your wrongdoing. Don't ignore God's warnings. There are consequences, and sometimes—like with Jim's wife's burns—those consequences can leave scars and cause lasting damage to those we love.

Someday the time will come when you'd give anything to go back and do those days over again. Don't look back with regrets. Heed God's warnings and avoid those sharp jolts of life.

Watch ye, stand fast in the faith,
quit you like men, be strong.
—*1 Corinthians 16:13*

Lord, help me to listen when you send warnings to me. You made me, so you understand that sometimes I don't pay attention as I should. Pinpoint the dangers in my spiritual life. Open my eyes and send zaps of conviction when I need them. And when those come, help me to pay attention to those words that you say to me in love. Help me to realize that you only want what's best for me. Keep me from decisions that will harm my testimony and those I love. Most of all, keep me from mistakes that will harm my relationship with you. Help me to look back at my life with gratefulness for your warnings instead of regrets that I didn't heed them. Amen.

THE BUILDING PERMIT PAGE

WHAT WILL I PERMIT GOD TO DO IN MY LIFE?

1. God sends warnings to us when we are getting ready to wander into dangerous circumstances spiritually. Have you been sensitive to his warnings, or have you just gone ahead and ignored them?

2. Jim didn't pay attention to the warnings and suffered serious consequences. Can you think of a time God zapped you with conviction about something? How did that affect you?

3. Do you need to spend more time reading the instructions in God's Word? What can you do to be more consistent with your Bible reading and your prayer time?

4. What can you do to protect those you love from experiencing those shooting-sparks moments of life?

TWENTY-ONE

THE KNEEPADS

Kneepads are used to cushion the knees when kneeling on hard surfaces like concrete or gravel. They're valued by builders in trades such as masonry, tile work, and plumbing. Quality kneepads grip well, are lined for comfort, and are suitable for working on delicate surfaces. Knee pads aren't much use unless they're adjustable and made to fit you. Make sure that you get the kind with thick cushioning and foam padding. Your knees will thank you.

Behind every work of God
you will always find some kneeling form.

—Dwight L. Moody

Humbling Yourself before God

Our knees are amazing. They allow us to walk, run, dance, bounce, move, and kneel. But like all of creation, they wear down. They stretch, loosen, and lack the agility they once had. We all wish it weren't so, but the march of years has a way of pulling out the props from our cherished hopes of eternal health.

Thankfully, there are kneepads. Carpet installers would be extremely uncomfortable without them. And you might find kneepads helpful when working on a project in the shop. Work that requires you to get on the ground and cut or carve. Even an under-the-sink plumbing project can be made more manageable if you have something between your kneecap and the hard floor. You and your loved one might use them when gardening to keep the hard, cold ground from creeping into your bones. And when the grandkids are around, you may use a knee protector when you help the wee ones with a bath.

There are many ways kneepads can come in handy. But how often do we use them because we've been praying so long and so fervently that we need their protection for our creaking cartilage? The answer is probably "not enough." How you choose to pray is irrelevant. Some like to sit, some kneel at the foot of their bed, some cuddle on the couch with children, and some stand with friends and neighbors at church. The substance matters, not the posture.

We each have multiple opportunities to speak to our heavenly Father every day. And when we see things going from bad to worse, we should take the position of prayer—and hit our knees. There's no other way to savor the assurance that you are dialed into God. Prayer brings both peace and power when you've all but given up hope.

Years ago many churches had kneelers, small benches that could be pulled from between the pew legs, which allowed the congregation to hit the ground for heartfelt prayer. Today we might not be so formal, but our hearts should still offer up a reverent posture of prayer. If this means kneeling, all the better. If your knees scream, *No way!* that's fine too. It's the attitude of seeking the Lord's face and grace that makes all the difference.

No matter the project, the next time you take advantage of the comfort of those kneepads, take some time to bow your heart. Capture a moment and put aside all the things you want to—need to—say, and quietly give yourself over to God's open arms, warm heart, and listening ear. He is waiting for you. And from whatever posture or position you choose, He will respond with love and sincerity.

THE BUILDING PERMIT PAGE

WHAT WILL I PERMIT GOD TO DO IN MY LIFE?

1. How do you know when you should be spending more time in prayer? Does it take hardship (a financial situation, family problems, or a prodigal child) to drive you to your knees?

2. Have you ever been a part of a full-fledged miracle (large or small)? What were you praying about—and what did God do for you?

3. Kneepads can often help a builder tolerate a difficult situation so he can keep working without extreme discomfort. How does time in prayer—time on your knees (figuratively or literally)—help you endure the hardships of life?

4. How often do you read or offer up the Lord's Prayer? What moves you most about this prayer of Christ?

TWENTY-TWO

THE HAMMER

A carpenter's hammer has a wood or fiberglass handle, a round steel head for pounding nails, and a claw for removing them. Hammers used by brick masons are square instead of round. The hammer is one of the most indispensable tools in the toolbox because it's used for so many things—from major projects such as building a house to simple tasks such as hanging pictures or mirrors. Hammers can be used to build things—or to destroy them.

Be wise in the use of time.
The question of life is not,
"How much time have we?"
The question is,
"What shall we do with it?"
—Anna Robertson Brown

USING YOUR TIME WISELY

Jeremy was primed and ready to work on the basement steps. He had his overalls on, a sturdy hammer, and a bag of nails. He picked up the first nail, stuck it in place on the board, and painstakingly hammered it into the wood.

Then he picked up another nail and went through the same process again. For hours. Over and over again, until his arm was sore and the bag was empty. Most of the nails were flush with the wood, but there were others that would have to be removed because they'd gone in crooked and would be a stumbling hazard to anyone who walked on the steps.

This process went on for days, and then weeks. Jeremy didn't quit, but observers wouldn't have noticed any progress on the building project from his efforts—despite all his hard work.

I guess this would be a good place to mention that Jeremy was three years old at the time. We were in the process of building our new home, and he wanted to be part of it. It was a great way to keep him busy while we worked on the framing or the finish work.

Our little guy loved it and would work with his hammer for hours. And the bottom two steps of our basement stairs are proof of that, as they are almost solid with nails.

But you know what? All of that hammering, all of those

countless hours of pounding nails into the boards, didn't make any difference when it came to the actual building of our home. They didn't connect two boards together, and they didn't hold the studs or trusses in place. They were just there.

They didn't have a purpose, and all that energy was basically wasted time.

Jeremy was just a little guy, so we'd expect that from him, but many of us do the same thing with our spiritual lives—and we're men who should know better.

God places a task on our hearts. But we're too busy spending our time on things that don't really matter. He shows us something in our lives that we need to fix. But we tell Him we'll do it later. Our Father says, *I want you to spend time with me!* But we're too busy collecting things and accumulating wealth or power.

You know, none of us will take a U-Haul with us when it comes our time to die. The real estate, the fancy cars and boats, the money in our bank accounts—not one bit of it will matter to us then.

Guys, are you spending your time wisely? Sharing the gospel with those who haven't heard? Leaving a legacy of faith behind for your family and others whose lives have touched yours?

Are you spending your time on things that will matter for eternity?

So teach us to number our days,
that we may apply our hearts unto wisdom.
—*Psalm 90:12*

Lord, I realize time is a precious gift and that no matter how much I wish I could, I can't go back and rewind the past to do it over again. Help me to make wise choices with my time. I realize you have specific tasks for me to do and that you've given me the talents to do them. I don't want to look back at the end of my days and see that I let you down, that I wasted the gifts and skills that you gave me. Help me to live each day in a manner where my children and future generations will remember a man who loved God, a man who gave willingly of his time to serve Him. Amen.

THE BUILDING PERMIT PAGE

WHAT WILL I PERMIT GOD TO DO IN MY LIFE?

1. Jeremy was a child, and he did what one would expect from a child. But many of us stay at a childlike level spiritually. We don't grow and mature. What do we need to adjust now so that we end our lives having done what truly matters?

2. Time is a precious commodity. Think of three ways you've wasted your time in the past spiritually. And then ask God to help you do things differently in the future.

3. Think of three goals you'd like to accomplish for God. And then ask Him to be the keeper of your schedule so you can do those tasks.

4. How will your family and future generations describe you? Will they remember a godly man who put God first?

TWENTY-THREE

THE AWL

An awl is a hardened steel rod sharpened to a point. The tip is often beveled for digging through difficult mediums. It is virtually unbreakable. The rod is fastened to a sturdy blocklike handle. It is used for making marks or punching small holes in wood, metalwork, and leather. Though simplistic in design, in experienced hands the awl is an extremely versatile tool.

When God uses His awl of salvation
and places His mark on us,
it's guaranteed to last through eternity.

—Michelle Cox

ON THE MARK

In the world of tools, a small standard awl has one very practical purpose: to save the integrity of your favorite pocketknife (or maybe your wife's favorite paring knife). Here's how. Instead of breaking off the thin tip of a pocket knife, an awl can be used to make small circular cuts for various purposes. By tapping in a handy pilot hole, for example, it's much easier to drive a nail or start a screw. The awl can also poke out a spot in sheetrock to place an anchor. And we've all experienced the need to add just one more hole to our straining leather belts, right? The uses for the awl are as varied as the user's imagination.

The stitching awl is used by skilled artisans for manipulating leather and other unwieldly fabrics to make shoes or bind books by hand. By contrast, a scratch awl does what its name implies. It marks a thin line, or even an intricate pattern, onto wood that then serves as the guide for a cutting tool that will follow along that etched pathway. This is called "scribing" a line. Without such a marker, the sawing done later won't be nearly as detailed. Think about how the scribes of old carefully transcribed Scripture onto paper. Without their single-minded devotion, we might not have the priceless beauty of God's Word today.

One caveat should be considered regarding the awl. Once it has been used and the hole or stroke has been decisively made, there's no taking it back. It's permanent. We must live with the decision to place *that* mark in *that* specific spot.

Our lives are filled with markers. From the time we were children and carried our grades home, we've become accustomed to others judging us. Remember having Mom or Dad sign the report card and carrying it back to the teacher? We learned early on that others were keeping track of us, evaluating us, making sure that we were on the mark. Though such attention grates at the time, in all honesty we need those markers to keep us safe and moving in the right direction.

As believers, having chosen to take on the mark of Christ can provide us with incomparable strength. Like an awl's alteration, our decision to accept the gift of salvation stays with us forever. The ingrained sign on our soul survives even our own self-deceptions, fears, and mind games.

This is because we are God's workmanship—in every pore, every detail, every thought, and every action. He has formed us and breathed life into us. He leaves His mark as both evidence and a reminder that we are His. And knowing that we can always lean on Him, even in the most difficult circumstances, reminds us of the permanency of that amazing love.

Then his master shall bring him unto the judges;
he shall also bring him to the door, or unto
the door post; and his master shall bore
his ear through with an aul;
and he shall serve him for ever.
—Exodus 21:6

Oh Lord, you have marked me in many ways. I look back and realize you have directed me toward many turning points. Times when I had the opportunity to choose to serve or to take what I thought I deserved. And I have smudged myself by many of my choices. When I could have done more for you, I chose to do less. Please forgive me for my weaknesses, and help me learn from them. I need to because I make mistakes so often. Your salvation gives me hope. Ultimately, the marks of your ownership are clear and obvious. But I must choose to see them to truly honor you. Amen.

THE BUILDING PERMIT PAGE

WHAT WILL I PERMIT GOD TO DO IN MY LIFE?

1. How does the watching world know that you belong to Jesus Christ? How are you marked for His service?

2. What does it mean to lead by serving? Provide examples you've witnessed of servant leadership in action. What are ways that you can serve others? Make a list of three things you can do and then put your plan into action.

3. What are the warning signs that you're serving other things instead of God, and what can you do to bring your attention back to Him?

4. List some opportunities for growth in your life. What are specific ways that you can draw closer to God and improve your spiritual walk?

TWENTY-FOUR

THE FLASHLIGHT

The builder uses a flashlight to brighten a dim corner, look up a chimney, or illuminate his way through a darkened basement. Flashlights come in all sizes and colors. Some are small, others are large, and some even come with a strobe light. There are powerful flashlights and others that just cast a dim light. They are available on phones, can be strapped around our heads for hands-free use, and can even be included as part of an ink pen or keychain—but all of them have to be recharged, or they require new batteries to keep them operating well.

One light in the darkness will make a difference, but when we all join together, we can light up our world.
—Michelle Cox

LIGHTING THE DARKNESS

Paul is a masonry contractor. When he estimates jobs for customers, one of the tools that he considers a must-have is his trusty flashlight. When he looks at a chimney for a homeowner, Paul often climbs into the attic to see if the bricks have deteriorated or if there are leaks. Or sometimes he has to look in dark basements for structural problems in homes.

If he has to crawl underneath a house, Paul can use a headlamp, a flashlight attached to a strap that goes around his head and keeps his hands free. When he wears it, that light can show issues with the piers or foundation. It can also help him see if there are rodents, snakes, spiders, or other wild animals under the home—always a good thing to see *before* you have an unexpected encounter.

There have been times when the batteries were dead or Paul forgot his flashlight—and he missed important details that cost him time and money. So it's important for him to make sure that he always has a flashlight in his truck and that the batteries are new or charged.

It's the same way with us spiritually. In John 8:12, Jesus said, "I am the light of the world: he that followeth me shall not walk in darkness, but shall have the light of life." He's our flashlight as we go about our lives each day. Here are some things we can ask God to illuminate for us as we spend time in His Word, in prayer, and in quiet times where we can listen to Him:

- Help me to see *you*, Lord. Remind me to reflect on who you are and your mighty power. Let me truly see what you've done for me and how you walk beside me each day.

- Help me to see *me*. Highlight the dark areas in my life that need repair. Pinpoint the places where I'm weak, and show me what I need to do to be strong and productive for you.

- Help me to see *others*. Give me a heart of compassion so that I'll look at other people with your eyes. Show me friends, loved ones, and strangers who need to hear about you.

- Help me to see the *path* you've chosen for me. Light the way, and don't let me take one step away from the plan that you have mapped out for me.

Just as the contractor needs to keep his batteries charged and his flashlight close at hand, we should be primed and ready for God to use us. And then we can shine our light into a dark world that needs to see Him.

Let your light so shine before men,
that they may see your good works,
and glorify your Father which is in heaven.
—*Matthew 5:16*

Lord, just as the builder uses his flashlight to shine into crevices and dark corners, use your light to shine into the dark and hidden places in my heart. Bring things to light that I need to change. Just as Paul uses the beam of his flashlight to expose hidden dangers, shine your light on situations where I need to be careful. Put a spotlight on areas where I can work to become more like you. I want to be a powerful light for you. Our world is a dark place with crime, national security issues, and people who would harm us. Those folks need to see you! I want to shine your love into the lives of others so that they may discover the precious light of the world. Amen.

THE BUILDING PERMIT PAGE

WHAT WILL I PERMIT GOD TO DO IN MY LIFE?

1. Paul uses his flashlight to illuminate what he needs to see when estimating or working on jobs. God describes His Word as a "lamp" (Psalm 119:105). How can spending time in your Bible show you the things in your life that you need to change?

2. Sometimes we turn off the God-light because we don't want Him to highlight things in our lives. Have you ever been guilty of that? How did it affect you?

3. Do you worry about finding direction for your life? Have you tried to feel your way through instead of asking Him to light your path? Take time to pray about the plans God has for you.

4. How do you think it would change us if we saw ourselves and others through His eyes?

TWENTY-FIVE

THE STUD FINDER

A stud finder is a tool that helps a builder easily find the studs hidden inside a wall. When hanging cabinets, bookshelves, and other heavy objects, it's important to anchor them to the studs for support, or the weight of the items will pull them from the wall, posing a potential safety hazard. Some stud finders use magnets to locate nails beneath the surface. Others are equipped with a spotlight system for pinpointing and locating the area of hidden strength.

A wise builder uses a stud finder to encounter nails in the studs. A wise man uses God's Word to encounter nail-scarred hands.

—Michelle Cox

135

Looking Past the Obvious

Knock knock. Can you hear it? The hollow thud versus the reassuring solid thump?

It takes talent—trying to find a two-by-six in the wall with your knuckle and ear. Some guys probably prefer pulling the blueprints to locate where the studs hide beneath the sheetrock, plaster, paint, and paper. We've all tried to tap in a nail (or many nails!) to hang a heavy frame or mirror. Finding that strong spot is vital.

Hanging a calendar or small picture is one thing, but if you need to put up a shelf or towel rack, a magnetic stud finder is light-years ahead of using your secret knock. The idea behind this handy device is that a strong magnet reveals where the nails are—the ones used to place the studs. So you get a solid hint about where you're gonna hit a thick chunk of wood. And that's exactly what you want. An anchor. You must fasten your nails, screws, cabinets, and TV into solid wood. Or else.

Even more high-tech is the spotlight stud finder. For less than twenty bucks, this device can locate the exact center of the beam and provide the gentleman with a hammer a zone of safety to pound away. It also shows exactly where the hot wires are beneath the wall so you aren't shocked by a lurking electrical nest.

From a spiritual perspective, we should always seek

that solid place where we can cling, even dangling from our fingertips when necessary. God offers us many spots of safety and shelter. He's that solid beam behind the wall, standing firmly in place—ready for us when we need Him. Perhaps we should reach out for help more often.

What are some ways to find that safe tower of strength? Look first in God's Word. You'll locate life-changing truths. Inside the cover of your Bible, you'll find freedom and hope. All you need to do is open it. No fancy locators are required, although you might want a concordance or your favorite online Bible search tools when you're ready to dig deeper.

You can also find hope and help by tapping into a wise Christian friend or by taking time to speak with your pastor. There are many small-group opportunities available in homes, at your place of worship, or even on the Web. And you can expand the body of Christ exponentially by sharing the truth with your neighbors and coworkers. Jesus Christ is Lord and Savior! That's still great news—especially in an ever-darkening world.

It all comes down to your willingness to see beyond the surface. To look past what's staring you in the face. God is calling you to a deeper commitment. Draw closer to Him, and without a doubt, He will draw closer to you.

And ye shall seek me, and find me,
when ye shall search for me with all your heart.
—*Jeremiah 29:13*

Father, sometimes I don't see what's right in front of me. I'm surprised at how much I miss. Despite all the treasure buried in your Word, I don't always bother to search for it. I'm satisfied with whatever can be easily gleaned from the surface, from chapter headings and sermon notes. Please show me how to go deeper in my spiritual walk. Lift my faith out of the day-to-day mire and let me see the full blueprint. Show me that life isn't merely about the here and now, but about every precious soul we can reach for God. Heaven is the ultimate goal—and reward. No matter what is raging in our families, nation, and world, remind us that only the things we do for you will matter. Open my eyes to the truth. Please, Lord, I need you. Amen.

THE BUILDING PERMIT PAGE

WHAT WILL I PERMIT GOD TO DO IN MY LIFE?

1. Does God need to pinpoint areas of your life that you think you have well hidden? Is He your day-to-day support, or are you trying to live life without Him?

2. Just as studs provide a strong surface for hanging things, God is our strong surface for life. How does that affect you?

3. What are some ways you can find that spiritual tower of strength in your life? How can you help provide that strength for others?

4. Recall a long-term goal you achieved. What role did seeking God's direction have in your success? How would the situation have been different if you hadn't sought God's guidance?

TWENTY-SIX

THE SQUARE

Made from one piece of steel, the square is an instrument for drawing or testing angles, and it can determine if a surface is flat. Often used for framing and roofing, the square is useful to mark patterns for things like stairway risers. Consistent use of the square when building a house ensures that corners will be square, windows and doors will fit properly, and store-bought cabinets can be installed without major difficulties. But if the builder tries to rush things and doesn't use the square as he should, multiple problems will arise in the years ahead.

Rushing ahead of God doesn't make the job get done faster, it just means that you've taken the task out of his hands and placed it in your far less capable ones.
—*Michelle Cox*

NO SHORTCUTS HERE

Dennis had never built a house before, but he'd done some research using home-building sites on the Internet, and he was confident he could do it. He started late in the summer, so he knew he had to move fast to complete the project before the winter weather hit the mountain area where he lived.

Dennis called a contractor acquaintance to bring his laser level to help square up the pegs for the foundation footings. When he learned it would be weeks before the man could work him into the schedule, Dennis decided he could just mark the dimensions on the ground and eyeball the lines so they looked straight.

It was a decision he would regret, one that affected his house from top to bottom. Throughout every stage of the building process, issues arose. When the carpenters came to build the walls and they pulled out their squares, there were complications in every room. Windows didn't hang right. It cost Dennis money every winter because the doors and windows didn't fit tightly and cold air blew through the cracks. And the problems continued for the thirty years he lived in his house.

Dennis still cringed when he thought of the wallpaper he'd tried to hang. There was no way to match the pattern,

and it looked so bad that he'd finally just taken it down and painted instead.

He'd been reminded of that out-of-square issue again when he'd had a builder, Carl, come out to measure for new cabinets and countertops in the kitchen.

Carl wrote down his measurements and pulled out his square. Then he scratched his head as he stood back and looked at the walls. "Whew, I don't think I've ever seen a house this out of square. We're going to have a doozy of a time trying to get these cabinets and countertops in. We can fix it, and it will be beautiful when it's done, but it's going to take way more time and money than it would have if everything were square."

Guys, when we take shortcuts spiritually, there are going to be problems. Instead of waiting on God, rushing ahead of Him can cost us. Oh sure, sometimes we can go back and make rough fixes to things at a later date, but there are consequences.

Just as doors don't fit tightly in an out-of-square house, an out-of-square man won't fit tightly with his Savior. And just as others looked at that messed-up wallpaper, people we care about will look at us and see the flaws.

It's much easier to walk the line for what God wants us to do and to make sure our hearts are squared up to Him than it is to live with the aftermath.

But they that wait upon the LORD shall renew
their strength; they shall mount up with wings as
eagles; they shall run, and not be weary;
and they shall walk, and not faint.
—*Isaiah 40:31*

Lord, I'm so often impatient. I have a dream on my heart or I get in the middle of a situation and I try to fix things myself. I get in a hurry and I don't wait on you. And I'll admit it—sometimes I get frustrated with you because you don't move as fast as I think you should. But Father, I've learned the hard way that when I don't wait on you, I make a mess of things. Remind me that even though I don't see you at work on my behalf, it doesn't mean you aren't busy behind the scenes. Help me not to settle for second best of my own doing, but to wait for you to put the pieces in place for the perfect plan you have for me. Amen.

THE BUILDING PERMIT PAGE

WHAT WILL I PERMIT GOD TO DO IN MY LIFE?

1. Dennis wasn't knowledgeable and was in too much of a rush when he should have taken the time to square up his house. Sometimes we do the same as Christians. How have you rushed God?

2. Just as there were consequences that Dennis discovered because of his unwise decision, there are consequences when we rush God. What have you learned from those times?

3. For those of us with fixer-upper personalities, it's sometimes hard to let go and let God fix things instead of us launching out on our own to do it. What's going on in your life right now that you need to turn over to Him?

4. Find three verses about waiting on God. What benefits can you discover when you don't push Him to meet *your* schedule?

TWENTY-SEVEN

THE EXTENSION CORD

Extension cords are used to connect a tool or appliance into a power receptacle. These flexible electrical power cables give you the freedom and convenience to work up to 300 feet away from the main household plug-in. However, the farther one gets from the outlet, the lower the carrying capacity of the current. As Christians, the farther we get away from God, the weaker we become in our Christian walk. Unhooking from our spiritual strength and support causes all sorts of long-term struggles.

Power depends on good connections—the train with the locomotive, machinery with the engine, the electrical mechanism with the powerhouse. And in the Christian life the follower of Jesus with the Spirit of Jesus.

—S. D. Gordon

PLUGGING INTO THE SOURCE

The smiling boy opened his junior toolbox. It was sturdy plastic and snapped open and shut. Just like Daddy's, only smaller. He looked through it until he found what he needed. His eyes widened as he revved up his plastic drill.

The tip of the battery-powered toy twirled. Faster and faster it spun as the child squeezed the trigger. For days he had delighted in the noisy, whirring tool, running from project to project, "fixing" a chair here, a doghouse there. But now it sputtered, barely turning.

Shoulders drooping, he carried it to his dad. The verdict was clear: dead batteries. His father helped him load fresh ones.

"I wish it wouldn't always stop," the boy said. He held out his hands expectantly.

"When you get older, I'll show you how to use my tools. You'll be able to hook right into the power source with an extension cord."

The boy nodded and ran off, drilling with determination. He didn't understand what Daddy meant, but it didn't matter. He trusted him.

His father put up sheetrock for a living. He knew his tools. Battery-powered drills can provide more mobility but often spend a significant amount of time recharging.

When they work, they make jobs easier, but when unavailable they only teach patience. That's why the cord plugged straight into the outlet is preferable.

Strange, isn't it? When we don't bother to plug into our personal energy source, we still dare to wonder why nothing works right. Prayer and Scripture—our spiritual extension cords—prompt the power flow. Without them, our strength quickly fails. God is the one true source that we desperately need at all times and in all places. And we *must* stay connected.

Extension cords allow us to work far from an outlet. The farther we get, however, the lower the carrying capacity of the current. A 16-gauge extension cord shorter than 50 feet long can power a 1625-watt tool, but a longer cord of the same gauge can't do the job. To stay safe, we must be careful about pushing the limits.

Our spiritual journey is the same. The farther a man moves from the Father, the weaker his power flow will be. For example, we may be doing His work and yet stretch ourselves too far. Our service to the Savior slackens because we're pushing too hard. Soon we find our strength and patience level at the danger point.

An overheated, overused extension cord can fray and start a fire. If someone touches even a single exposed strand of a damaged wire, a burn will result.

We must draw strength from God daily. It's how

we get through the challenges of life. Make sure you're closely connected to Him so your loved ones won't ever have to face a jolting shock from someone who's not well grounded.

I am the vine, ye are the branches:
He that abideth in me, and I in him,
the same bringeth forth much fruit:
for without me ye can do nothing.
—*John 15:5*

Lord, help me to see ways I've distanced myself from you. What I need most is to stay close to you and to be secure in your power and strength. And yet, like an untrained apprentice, I dangerously push my limits. I don't want to run down and falter. But to stay connected, I know I must pray and read my Bible. Please show me how to incorporate you into my day. Keep my mind and thoughts on you. Help me to remember and count the many blessings you have showered down upon me. Replace my weakness with your constant flowing strength. And most of all, make me the kind of man my children can be proud of. Give me many opportunities to point them to you. Amen.

THE BUILDING PERMIT PAGE

WHAT WILL I PERMIT GOD TO DO IN MY LIFE?

1. We often take for granted the power we have through our connection with Jesus. Why do we repeatedly try to go it alone when we can receive strength from our awesome Savior?

2. What happens when you forget to plug into your one true power source? How differently does your day go when you pause for a quiet time, reflection, and prayer before taking on the challenges of the day?

3. What strength do you gain from staying close to the Savior? List some of the ways God has proven Himself faithful.

4. How could you change your routine to assure access to that needed nearness? What are some ways you can plug into God throughout the day, no matter where you are?

TWENTY-EIGHT

THE PLANE

The plane is a hand tool that is used for trimming doors, loosening drawers, and other tasks where smoothing off rough edges is needed. Though considered "old-fashioned" today, it is still invaluable for shaping, smoothing, and straightening wood. Depending on the job, a larger bench plane may work best while a block plane is best for smaller areas. This tool doesn't work well when the blade is dull so keeping the blade smooth and sharp will allow you to do your very best work.

God's love won't shine through unless
He removes the parts of us that obstruct
others from seeing Him.
—John Perrodin

SMOOTHING THE ROUGH EDGES

Construction requires multiple steps and stages. Along the way to final inspections, progress may be noted, but every real man knows that a job isn't finished until the big boss—a.k.a. your better half—says it meets her high standards. You certainly understand where she's coming from.

Undoubtedly, you've done a project with a friend or family member where you didn't see eye to eye on quality control. In other words, while your pal was packing his tools in anticipation of a plate of nachos and the big game, you were noting the rough spots on the cabinet that still needed leveling and touch-up. So you pulled out your faithful plane and kept working. Smiling, you directed your friend to the chips, cheese, salsa, and TV—no hard feelings—and kept at it. Finishing. Perfecting.

You've probably had the same sort of experience when you asked a child or grandchild to pick up their toys, wash the car, or clean up after the dog. When you went to inspect the work, you discovered some, um, *discrepancies* in quality and called for an immediate do-over. You can't offer your stamp of approval unless the job is done right.

God looks at us the same way. Imagine Him watching us admire our physique in the mirror. What muscles. What strength. What power. He probably chuckles. Even ignoring our superficial emphasis, He can't help but notice a few zillion glaring rough edges. He still loves us, but He wants us to realize that the Christian journey is just that. We're simply not fit for heaven while still on earth. It doesn't work that way.

As we strive to improve, our main emphasis needs to be on our spiritual growth and advancement. Of course, we should care for the body God gave us, but strengthening our soul is of utmost importance.

This is why we often feel the pinching, piercing edge of God's plane as He works to smooth out the rough spots in our character, carve away at the selfishness clinging to our hearts, or strip down the gunk clogging our spiritual core. In all honesty, we shouldn't want it any other way. Unless God takes away the parts of us that obstruct others from seeing Him, His love won't come through. All that the lost and dying will see is us—when we really want them to focus on the Savior.

At times, the shaping process hurts, tears at our heart. The plane bites through thin skin. Things get jostled, especially our pride, our goals, our desire to come first in the eyes of others. But we're not quitters, especially when we know that the Master Craftsman stands ready to take us to a higher level of service.

Every valley shall be filled, and every mountain and hill shall be brought low; and the crooked shall be made straight, and the rough ways shall be made smooth.

—*Luke 3:5*

Lord, I feel as though I spend the better part of my days overcoming obstacles. Some are small and almost laughable, but others hold me captive for many minutes or hours. I want to get on with things, but I'm trapped, unable to proceed because there are so many messes to clear out before I can take a single step forward. Smooth my rough edges, Lord. Clear the way for me. Assure me I'm on the right path. I admit my desires are often driven by selfishness. I don't like being held back, and yet I often am. Teach me what I need to learn from the detours, the deep valleys, the slow slogs upward. Show me the way you've chosen for me. No matter how hard the climb, help me conquer the mountains you've set before me. Smooth my route in your perfect timing. Amen.

THE BUILDING PERMIT PAGE

WHAT WILL I PERMIT GOD TO DO IN MY LIFE?

1. Shaping rough edges spiritually can be uncomfortable, but that's how God develops and defines the character in our lives. Think of three times God has had to do this for you. What did you learn from those moments?

2. How often do you take the time to help others move ahead in the game of life? Or is it usually all about *your* goals, dreams, and desires?

3. Quality control is an important aspect of any worksite. How can you develop quality in your spiritual life so you become a man after God's heart?

4. List some of the good gifts God has provided for you. What are the best ways to sharpen these amazing tools God has granted you?

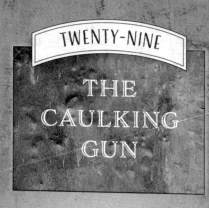

TWENTY-NINE

THE CAULKING GUN

A caulking gun is used to seal surfaces so unwanted elements don't infiltrate and cause damage. The builder uses different types of caulk for different purposes, but to be useful, the caulk must be used in conjunction with the caulking gun. Knowing how much pressure to use and having a steady hand while using the caulking gun can make all the difference in the quality of the finished task.

The hand that holds the caulking gun
rules the quality of the work, and the hand
that holds the man rules the quality of his life.
—*Michelle Cox*

WHO'S IN CONTROL?

Bill sighed in frustration. He'd never done remodeling work before. It had looked so easy when he was watching the how-to video on YouTube. His dad had done numerous DIY projects through the years. He'd offered to give him a hand, but Bill had wanted to do it himself, so he turned down the offer.

His first mistake was in buying a cheap caulking gun. Yeah, that had been a lesson in frustration. Instead of leaving behind a smooth line of caulk to fill in the cracks by the molding, he'd ended up with an unsightly mess because the caulk kept flowing out of the tube.

He went online and read reviews for caulking guns. After reading multiple comments that said that paying more for one would be worth it in the long run, he invested in a better model.

Bill's second mistake came because he didn't realize there are different types of caulk for different tasks. He'd wasted several tubes of caulking before he realized it wasn't the right kind of sealant for the crack beside the bathtub.

His third mistake came from not using the caulking gun properly. As he quickly discovered, the hand that controlled it was the most important thing. A more experienced handyman would have known exactly how much pressure to put on the trigger and how long to maintain that pressure.

And as Bill later admitted to his wife, his biggest mistake by far had come from not letting his father take charge of the job.

Guys, how many times have we done the same thing? God says He'll help us, but we want to do things ourselves instead. We settle for second best when He has something so much better for us—and He's already paid the ultimate price for it.

God's designed each of us, and He has a unique purpose and plan for our lives. But like Bill using the wrong kind of caulking for the task, we often try to be like someone else because we're impressed with their fancy cars, big bank accounts, or shiny boats—instead of fulfilling the unique plan that God's designed for us.

God has offered to give us a hand—to be there with us—in all that we do. Just as with some of those handyman jobs, the process can sometimes be difficult as God seals the cracks and crevices in our lives where sin and wrongdoing creep in. But He knows just how much pressure to apply and how long to apply it so that He ends up with a man of quality instead of an unsightly mess.

Don't look back at the end of your days and realize that your biggest mistake came from not allowing God's hand to be in control of your life.

For I the LORD thy God will hold thy right hand,
saying unto thee, Fear not; I will help thee.
—Isaiah 41:13

Father, I so often make a mess of things. Instead of trusting you and allowing you to be in control of my life, I try to take things into my own hands. Help me to learn from my mistakes. I place myself in your hands today—in those hands that were nailed to a cross because you loved me so much that you died for me. Help me to remember there's no better place to be. Take your caulking gun of grace and seal those cracks and crevices where sin and doubt creep into my heart. Remodel my life into something of beauty for you. I love you, Lord, and I want you to be in complete control of everything I do. Amen.

THE BUILDING PERMIT PAGE

WHAT WILL I PERMIT GOD TO DO IN MY LIFE?

1. God uses different individuals for different tasks, but none of us can be useful without His hand guiding us. When was a time you had trouble letting Him be in control?

2. It's easy to let sin and doubt creep into our lives, especially when we aren't paying attention. What steps can you take to seal those cracks and crevices so undesirable elements don't affect you?

3. Using the right amount of pressure is vital when using a caulking gun. Think back to times in your life when God allowed you to experience pressure. What did you learn?

4. Bill made a mess when he tried to use the caulking gun. None of us want to look back someday and realize we made a mess of our lives. What can you do to avoid that?

THIRTY

THE TOOLBOX

A toolbox is a container used for storing tools to make them easier to locate and to reduce damage to the tools. A toolbox filled with tools can mean the difference between a well-maintained home and a home that is falling apart. However, the toolbox doesn't do any good unless it is picked up and used. Choosing a quality toolbox is also important. A poorly constructed one won't hold up to wear and tear, won't open easily, and will fall apart under pressure.

> The contents of the toolbox are only
> as good as the man who is using them.
>
> —*Michelle Cox*

WHAT'S IN YOUR TOOLBOX?

Albert had forgotten his toolbox. Again. As a contractor, he'd known he'd need his tools, but his mind had been on other things and he'd neglected to put the toolbox on the truck.

The things he'd been thinking about that morning were minor, but the toolbox was a necessity. His poor planning impacted his employees, as well, when work came to a screeching halt on the jobsite. The toolbox didn't do him any good just sitting in his basement.

We've all done boneheaded things like that. We do it spiritually as well, as our Bibles collect dust and we go for days without spending serious time in prayer. And sometimes we forget that neglecting our spiritual toolbox doesn't just impact us, it also touches the lives of those we love. Are we stocking our spiritual toolboxes with things that will matter for eternity, or are we distracted by other things?

My friend Lori Brown posted something on Facebook recently that provides a wonderful example of this:

My toolbox is nothing special to look at. It's just a plastic green toolbox. But it's what's inside that's special. When my twin sister and I bought our first house together, our dad decided that we needed a good toolbox to address all of our house needs.

Dad's parents were dairy farmers, so between my grandfather and my dad, we had a lot of tools around the farm. Although I didn't have the first clue what to do with any sort of tool, dad went to the store for me, bought a big toolbox, and filled it with hammers, screwdrivers, bolts, screws, and other stuff that I can't name.

My dad passed away recently. My toolbox is therefore more precious to me than before, because when I open it, I'm holding the hammer that dad used to build shelves for my closet, the screwdriver he used to put together my Barbie house, and the bolts and screws that once held my awards and pictures on the wall.

That toolbox is an extension of a father I loved deeply, a man who always took care of his girls. My toolbox represents a godly man with a servant's heart who always put other people first. I still don't know what to do with a screwdriver or a hammer, but my toolbox went up in value this year because of the memories.

I'm thankful for a dad who loved God and always took care of me.

Therefore, my beloved brethren, be ye stedfast,
unmoveable, always abounding in the work
of the Lord, forasmuch as ye know that
your labour is not in vain in the Lord.
—1 Corinthians 15:58

Father, remind me of the importance of my spiritual toolbox. Instill a deep love for your Word in my heart. Give me a hunger to spend time talking with you. Don't ever let me forget that others are watching to see how I live each day, and that my actions—whether good or bad—will leave an impact on them. Give me a servant's heart and a fierce love for you. Make me a man of bold character, a man who lives his life in such a manner that my footsteps will lead my children and others to you. Give me the legacy of a man who loved God and his family. Amen.

THE BUILDING PERMIT PAGE

WHAT WILL I PERMIT GOD TO DO IN MY LIFE?

1. What's the status of your spiritual toolbox? Is it filled with junk? What do you need to remove from your life? Make a list of things you can do to become a better man.

2. Lori's dad filled a toolbox for his daughters. He left behind memories of a dad who fixed things for them and loved them. He also left behind sweet memories of a dad who loved God. What legacy are you leaving for those you love? What will they remember about you?

3. Are you using the tools (the talents) God's given you, or are they going to waste? Name three talents you could use for God.

4. A toolbox is only as good as the man who is using it. Ask God to make you the man you desire to be.

Isn't it amazing how you can find
glimpses of God
on every item in your toolbox?
Whenever you use your toolbox,
remember this:
A man who builds his life on God's Word
will always be assured of a firm foundation.
God considers you a valuable tool in
His toolbox of souls.
Build your life based on His Word
and become a man of character for Him.

We would love to hear how these devotionals have touched and impacted your life. Please contact Michelle and John to share your thoughts and stories with us.

We promise to write back.

ACKNOWLEDGMENTS

Many people are involved in making a book become a reality, and we'd like to express our gratitude to them. Thanks so much to Carlton Garborg for catching the vision for *God Glimpses from the Toolbox* with us, and to David Sluka, Bill Watkins, Michelle Winger, Darcie Clemen, and the rest of the team at BroadStreet Publishing Group. It's been a joy working with you.

Thank you to Margaret Skiles and our beta readers who took the time to read our manuscript and came back with valuable suggestions and comments. You helped make our book better. Also, thank you to Lori Brown for allowing us to share her story in chapter 30.

There are no words to express our gratitude for our prayer team. You are the wind beneath our words, and we couldn't do what we do without you. We appreciate your prayers, your encouragement, and your willingness to pray for us and our work.

I (Michelle) would like to thank my coauthor, John Perrodin, for being the best coauthor in the world. Seriously.

You bring so much to our projects and make the experience enjoyable from start to finish.

I'd also like to thank my husband, Paul, for being my biggest cheerleader, praying for me, being my sounding board for ideas, and answering a gazillion questions about tools while I worked on this book. I love you, baby. You're an important part of all that I do. Thank you for allowing God to build you into such a special man.

I (John) have been blessed by having an amazing coauthor, Michelle Cox, who not only works harder than any writer I know, but also has believed in our *God Glimpses* concept for years. Literally. Thank you, Michelle. Your faithful fortitude and hopeful attitude have truly made this book a reality.

I am so grateful to my extremely handy wife, Sue. Your help has allowed us to tackle projects that boggled my mind at the time and gave us cause for great laughter afterward. You are amazing and I love you. Thanks, honey, for letting me see the Lord's tender heart through you.

Most importantly, we'd like to thank God for the idea for this book, for answering our prayers and sending inspiration as we started each chapter, and for allowing us to write for Him.

Finally, thanks so much to all of you—our readers. We prayed for you as we worked on *God Glimpses from the Toolbox*. We hope that the words will encourage your hearts and provide glimpses of Him, and that you'll become men of character who will impact your families and the world for God. Thank you for coming on this project in the tool-box with us.

ABOUT THE AUTHORS

JOHN PERRODIN

Since childhood, John has loved books and wanted to be a writer. A registered nurse, he works as a patient representative for Centura Health Services.

John coauthored *Simple Little Words* with Michelle Cox and the Renegade Spirit trilogy novels with Jerry B. Jenkins. An attorney, speaker, and journalist, he wrote *3-Minute Devotions for Grads* and contributed to various devotional volumes, including *The Spirit Calling*. He has also prepared Bible commentaries, written magazine articles, and personally mentored authors who want to improve their skills.

John has worked for Focus on the Family, Promise Keepers, Alliance Defending Freedom, the Jerry Jenkins Writers Guild, and Alive Literary Agency. He lives with his fantastic wife and remarkable children in Colorado.

MICHELLE COX

Known for her "encouragement with a Southern drawl," Michelle Cox is a speaker and an award-winning, best-selling author. She is a member of the blog team for *Guideposts.* Her "Life with a Southern Grandmother" column runs twice each week at www.Guideposts.org.

Michelle is a contributing writer for *Leading Hearts Magazine* and does reviews and interviews for ChristianCinema.com. She has written for FoxNews.com, Focus on the Family, *WHOA Magazine for Women,* and a variety of other publications and sites. Michelle has been a guest on numerous television and radio programs, including *Hannity* and *Focus on the Family.*

She is the creator of the Just 18 Summers® brand of parenting products and resources. Visit her at www.just-18summers.com, on Twitter @michelleinspire, and on Facebook at www.Facebook.com/MichelleCoxInspirations and www.Facebook.com/just18summers.

MORE GOD GLIMPSES

God Glimpses from the Jewelry Box
BECOMING JEWELS GOD CAN USE

What's in your jewelry box? A love letter, lock of hair, watch, or safety pin? Did you know that God's fingerprints—evidence of His presence—can be found there as well? We can uncover some amazing spiritual lessons tucked between our pearls, earrings, and silver bracelets.

Sometimes we act as if God is distant, but God glimpses are present in every aspect of our lives. We just have to look for them. Take a trip through thirty items in a jewelry box and discover encouragement, inspiration, and confirmation that God is so close we can reach out and touch Him.

Be bling for the King. Look for God glimpses in your jewelry box and shine for Jesus.